MUSCLE CARS

MUSCLE CARS

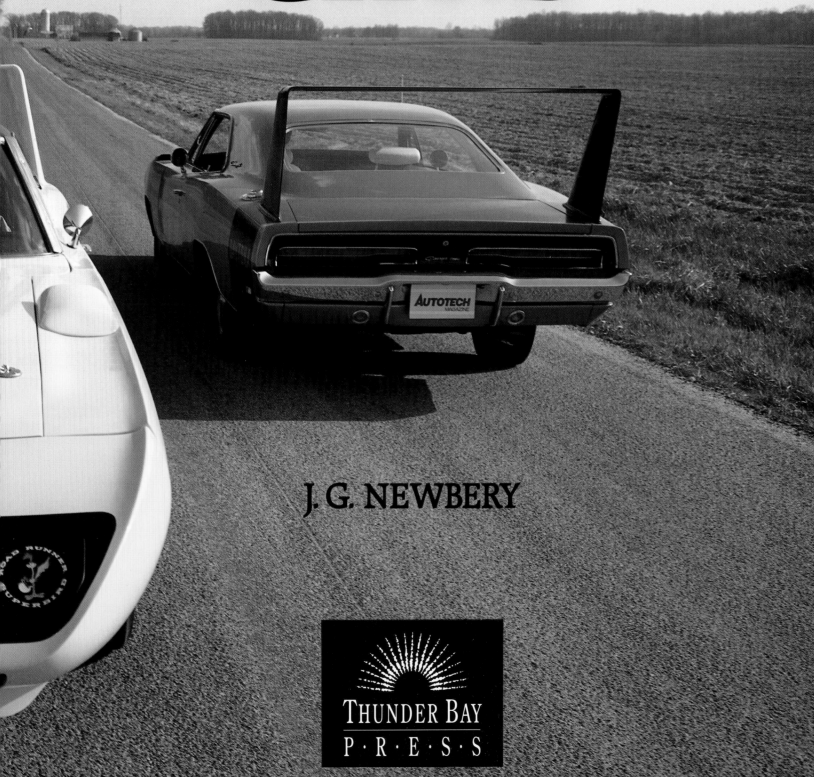

J. G. NEWBERY

THUNDER BAY
P·R·E·S·S

Published by
Thunder Bay Press
5880 Oberlin Drive, Suite 400
San Diego, California 92121

Produced by
Brompton Books Corporation
15 Sherwood Place
Greenwich, Connecticut 06830

Newbery, J. G.
    Muscle cars / J.G. Newbery.
        p.   cm.
    Includes index.
    ISBN 1-57145-007-6 : $19.98
    1. Muscle cars—United States—History.   I. Title.
TL23.N48   1994
629.222—dc20   94-19959
                                                              CIP

Printed in China

PAGE 1: Among Buick's later Muscle Cars was this 1970 GS convertible, with the hot Stage I power options on its 455-cubic-inch V8.

PAGES 2-3: Few Muscle Cars stood out like MoPar's winged wonders of 1969-70, the Plymouth Road Runner Superbird (LEFT) and Dodge Daytona (RIGHT).

THESE PAGES: Another 1969 Dodge Daytona, showing the characteristic bullet-nose and huge rear wing, designed for high-speed racing at NASCAR. This one has the legendary Hemi V8 under its hood.

Contents

Introduction

Between the early 1960s and the early 1970s, the American motor industry turned out an astonishing array of high-performance cars which has never been equaled. Most important, the cars weren't saddled with high sticker prices and aimed at the very wealthy, but were priced at the lower end of the market and were aimed at performance-crazy kids. These cars were the Muscle Cars. They offered excitement at affordable prices, and they were characteristic of the free-for-all, hedonistic era in which they were built. Today, they seem almost irresponsible – but back in the early 1960s the major issues of safety and exhaust emissions which color current perceptions of the automobile hadn't even swum into view.

Of course, there had been high-performance cars from Detroit long before the 1960s. Auto historians point to Oldsmobile's 1949 overhead-valve Rocket V8 as the motor which put America on course for the Muscle Car era. That was a high-output engine designed for the big Oldsmobiles, but when the division also put it into the smaller and lighter 88 models, what had been a family sedan suddenly started winning races.

Although overhead-valve V8s revolutionized the motor industry in the early 1950s, most makers didn't show much interest in producing high-performance sedans. Consequently, sedan races were mostly fought out between Oldsmobiles and Hudsons, which had nothing more exciting under their hoods than a big six-cylinder motor. It wasn't until 1955 and the Chrysler 300 that performance became an issue in the showrooms.

Even then, other automakers weren't unduly concerned by these big and fast sedans. The Chrysler 300 went through several model changes before another serious performance sedan appeared on the market in the shape of Ford's 1960 Starliner hardtop, which offered 360bhp from its 352-cubic-inch V8. In many ways, this was a turning point, because it was the first time any maker other than Chrysler had built a production engine with more than one brake horsepower per cubic inch – and even Chrysler's 1956 354 V8 hadn't exceeded that magic barrier quite so convincingly, with just 355bhp. It was when other automakers tried to outdo Ford that the Muscle Car era began.

LEFT: Hot machinery in the early 1950s meant sedans like this Hudson Hornet, with no more than 170bhp from its 308-cubic-inch in-line six.

TOP RIGHT: Cadillac's overhead-valve V8 opened up new performance possibilities for cars like this 1949 fastback model.

ABOVE RIGHT: More mid-fifties muscle: the Chrysler 300 was for many years acknowledged as the fastest sedan around. This is a 1955 300C, with a 300bhp, 331-cubic-inch V8.

What exactly is a Muscle Car?

It's not easy to define the term Muscle Car to everyone's satisfaction, not least because it has been misapplied so often over the years. One of the cars which has regularly been described as a Muscle Car is the Chevrolet Corvette – at least in its more potent, big-block, forms. The big-block Corvettes most certainly were high-performance cars, and many of them were all but unbeatable when set against other high-performance machinery; but they weren't really Muscle Cars. They are better classified as sportscars, and the distinction in the marketplace between a sportscar buyer and a Muscle Car buyer would have been very clear to any showroom salesman in the 1960s and early 1970s.

Muscle Cars started out as "sleepers" – ordinary-looking sedans in their lightest, two-door forms, packing high-horsepower big-block V8s which enabled them to outdrag unsuspecting victims when the stoplights turned green. Young performance enthusiasts rated that high on the fun scale. Before too long, though, a substantial proportion of buyers started demanding cars which *looked* tough as well as played tough, and so Detroit responded with racing stripes, high-visibility hood scoops, and a whole raft of other add-ons which advertised power and performance. It wasn't long after that when these add-ons were used to dress up lesser cars which didn't have the really brutal acceleration of the Muscle Cars proper, but real performance enthusiasts weren't fooled.

Somewhere along the line, Muscle Cars stopped being ordinary sedans, too. Buyers wanted something a little more stylish, and so the Muscle Car ranks swelled to accommodate convertibles and, above all, hardtop coupés. Not long after the first ponycars arrived, Detroit also started building editions of these which had all the high-performance ingredients of the sedan- or hardtop-based muscle machinery, and these, too, can be thought of as Muscle Cars.

The most important ingredient in any Muscle Car was undoubtedly acceleration. Total performance was not part of the equation, even though it was true that race-tuned versions of many top Muscle Cars could also storm around the superspeedways at 180mph or more in the hands of professional drivers. What buyers wanted was performance which could be used on the street in traffic-lights drag races, and performance which could be used at the dragstrip on weekends. That's why Muscle Car enthusiasts talk reverentially of zero to 60mph acceleration times and of quarter-mile times and trap speeds. Many Muscle Cars were capable of 130mph or more straight off the showroom floor, but those speeds meant very little to the average buyer because they were simply not usable on a regular basis.

The best Muscle Cars were those which were equally at home on street or strip, though many were biased toward one type of use or the other. Some of those which turned in the fastest quarter-miles were almost undriveable on the street because of the nature of their power delivery. And some of those which impressed on the street really weren't in the first division on the dragstrip. But the Muscle Car world had room for them both.

Obviously, no car without a powerful engine qualified

as a Muscle Car, although the amount of power necessary to produce dragstrip performance was relative. A small-block V8 in a light car could often equal the acceleration provided by a big-block V8 in a larger and heavier model. There was also more to Muscle Cars than their engines. Many had limited-slip differentials to prevent wheelspin under fierce acceleration; many had heavy-duty suspension with anti-tramp bars on the rear axle to help keep their rear wheels in full contact with the ground under maximum acceleration from rest; and enthusiasts still argue over the relative merits of four-speed stick shifts and automatics. In this area, however, one thing was clear: the massive torque put out by some of these engines needed heavy-duty drivetrain components if it wasn't going to destroy something whenever it was used in anger.

All the emphasis in these cars was on straight-line acceleration, of course, and very little was on handling or braking until quite late in the Muscle Car era. It's a plain fact that the brakes on many early and mid-period Muscle Cars were totally inadequate for everyday use, as they weren't uprated to match the engines. Equally, the huge big-block motors tended to make the intermediate models nose-heavy, which in turn could make them quite frightening to drive at speed over twisty roads. It wasn't until the Sports Car Club of America (SCCA) introduced its Trans Am racing series in 1966 that handling mattered even in racing. After that, it started to matter on the street as well, and in due course the safety lobby had its effect on brake specifications. By the end of the Muscle Car era, many of the high-performance cars were quite well-balanced in a way that was completely unknown to their predecessors.

In competition

It's debatable how important the major competitions were for Muscle Car sales. Throughout the Muscle Car era – and with periodic exceptions – all the major manufacturers except for General Motors continued to support NASCAR (National Association for Stock Car Auto Racing), which emphasised qualities of durability at very high speeds. Although successes at NASCAR made good publicity for the manufacturers, the young performance enthusiasts who bought Muscle Cars generally didn't drive at NASCAR speeds and didn't need cars which would achieve such impressive feats.

Nevertheless, the NASCAR authorities insisted that components used in the high-speed race cars had to be available (usually in relatively small numbers) through the showrooms as well, and this led to the creation of a number of interesting "homologation specials" which the Muscle Car fans lapped up. The best examples are the Dodge Charger Daytona and Plymouth Road Runner Superbird, which were fitted with huge aerofoils and bullet-noses for the NASCAR tracks and had to be sold through the showrooms in the same form. While the aerodynamic add-ons made no difference to performance on the street, their outrageous appearance undoubtedly added to the cars' street appeal.

More important were the NHRA's (National Hot Rod Association) quarter-mile events. These emphasised acceleration, which was what the Muscle Cars were all about, and Muscle Car owners could attempt to emulate the times set by the professionals when they went to their local dragstrips at weekends. There were, of course, different classes for stock cars and for modified examples, and so the most startling quarter-mile times

were out of reach of those who raced their everyday transport. But the NHRA's quarter-mile became a standard test of acceleration; the performance-car magazines faithfully tested every new Muscle Car for quarter-mile performance; and several manufacturers put money behind professional drivers who did well in NHRA events with highly modified versions of standard models.

Lastly, there was the SCCA's Trans Am series, which started in 1966 and became the showcase for ponycar racing until the major manufacturers pulled out in 1970. The importance of these events is well enough illustrated by the fact that several cars were named after them: Pontiac's top Firebird was actually called the Trans Am, for example, while Dodge fielded "T/A" performance editions of some of their cars. Without the Trans Am, performance enthusiasts would also have been denied Ford's Boss 302 Mustang and Chevrolet's Z-28 Camaro, both of which would have been sad omissions from the Muscle Car Hall of Fame.

Development of the Muscle Car

Muscle Cars didn't appear on the market as a fully-fledged phenomenon, and nor did they always conform to the same set of criteria. Over the years, they changed quite considerably, not only to meet customer expectations but also as their makers tried to offer more performance in packages which made them more profit.

The first Muscle Cars were full-size sedans with rip-snorting big-block V8s under their hoods. Big and heavy cars naturally needed powerful V8s to get them moving at respectable speeds, and so this was a natural outgrowth of existing product trends. But what changed the direction in which Muscle Cars would develop was Chrysler's dreadful mistake in 1962, when the corporation introduced some hideously ugly *smaller* Dodges and Plymouths and described them as full-size models. The styling was one mistake; the downsizing was another; but it didn't take long for Chrysler to recognize that these smaller and lighter cars could be given dragster-like acceleration when equipped with powerful big-block V8s.

It took a year or so for the message to sink in else-

LEFT: Early muscle models were low-key, but by the end of the sixties machinery like this Dodge Daytona left onlookers in no doubt about its performance pretensions.

ABOVE: The Trans Am race series gave Pontiac a name which they applied to their hottest Firebirds. By the time of this early 1970s model, power outputs were dropping, however.

RIGHT: Plymouth's Road Runner Superbird was a low-production variant of the budget-muscle Road Runner model.

where, and then the other automakers began to look at putting big-block engines into their intermediate ranges, which were similar in size to the Dodge and Plymouth models. First on the street was the 1964-model Pontiac GTO, and that car set a trend which all the major manufacturers were obliged to follow for the next eight to ten years. By the middle of the decade, full-size Muscle Cars had virtually ceased to exist.

The intermediates didn't have things all their own way, though. During 1964, Ford announced its new Mustang ponycar. Lighter and smaller than the intermediates, and with a sporty image, it was a natural for a high-performance engine – and that didn't have to be a vast and heavy big-block. The first hot Mustangs, including the famous 1965 Shelby models, got by very well with a small-block V8. Big-block models appeared rather later, but in the meantime, other manufacturers scrambled to produce hot ponycars in the Mustang's image.

Sensing the greatly increased competition, the Muscle Car makers started to look around for a formula which would put them ahead of the pack. It was Chrysler's Plymouth division who found it first, and put it into practice with the 1968-model Road Runner. The Road Runner was the first of the budget Muscle Cars – intermediates with powerful V8s, but fitted with as little non-essential equipment as possible in order to keep sticker prices down. For a couple of years, these cars were a runaway success with the youth muscle market.

Hot compacts were the next stage. In fact, their first appearance had been in 1968, when Dodge had announced the Dart GTS, but they didn't start to sell really strongly until 1970. Smaller and lighter than the intermediates, they didn't need big-block motors to give them exciting performance, and insurance companies looked more benignly on their small-block V8s than on

the huge and powerful big-blocks which had carried the Muscle Cars through the 1960s. The first really successful hot compact was the 1970 Plymouth Duster 340, although its success owed as much to external influences as to the excellence of its design.

Those external influences were the new Federal laws governing automative safety and exhaust emissions, which had first had their effect on the 1968 models. They added weight and, gradually, they strangled the power and torque outputs of the big-block V8s. By 1969 Detroit was having difficulty hiding from its customers what was happening, and sales of the traditional Muscle Cars took a serious tumble in 1970. Into the gap stepped the hot compacts, but there wasn't any doubt that the performance car market was dying. Over the next few years, hot compacts, hot intermediates and hot ponycars all struggled for survival. When fuel shortages came along in the winter of 1973-74 to compound America's automotive miseries, the Muscle Car era died.

ABOVE: Ford offered muscle versions of its Mustang ponycar, like this 1970 Boss 302 with 290bhp V8 under the hood.

LEFT AND RIGHT: The Pontiac GTO started a new trend in 1964, forcing Muscle Car makers to concentrate on intermediate-sized models. On the right is a 1966 convertible, with 389-cubic-inch V8. By the time of the 1969 hardtop (LEFT), the shape had changed dramatically and the engines were 350- or 400-cubic-inch types, but the affordable-performance image remained unchanged.

1961

Enter the 409

It would be hard to disagree with those who see the arrival of Chevrolet's 409-cubic-inch engine in the middle of the 1961 season as heralding the start of the Muscle Car era. Yet the division's planners could not have foreseen what they were starting when they gave the go-ahead for development of a new big-block V8 for their full-size models. All that really interested them at that stage was getting one over on arch-rivals Ford, whose new 390-cubic-inch engine was cleaning up at the dragstrips and grabbing some welcome publicity for its makers.

Chevrolet's counter to the Ford 390 was a bored-and-stroked version of their existing 348 big-block V8. The sales ploy which lay behind it was a shrewd one, based on the principle that if big is beautiful, bigger must be even more beautiful – and it worked. The new 409 had a clear 19 cubic inches of capacity more than the Ford, and that gave it instant status among the street-racing fraternity. Never mind that the most powerful versions of Ford's 390 put out 375bhp, which was significantly more than the 360bhp which the 409 could muster. Never mind that the Ford was pumping out 401bhp by the end of the season. To have a Chevy with the 409 badge on its fenders drew more admiration on the street and at the drive-in than any Ford with a 390 under its hood.

The 409 was available only in the sporty full-size Impala coupés and convertibles for 1961, and Chevrolet

BELOW LEFT: The performance addict's dream in 1961 was a Chevrolet Impala with the hot 409-cubic-inch motor under its hood – and what could be more stylish than this convertible version?

RIGHT: One of the hot Fords for 1961 was the Galaxie. This good-looking beast is the Starliner coupé, which had the 390 V8.

BELOW: Until 1961, performance had been pretty much the exclusive preserve of cars like Chevrolet's Corvette two-seater. But now, hot sedans began to attract as much interest as sportscars.

Muscle Car Choice – 1961

Chevrolet Impala SS 409
Ford Fairlane 500

backed it up with a new Super Sport trim package. This package was also available for Impalas with the regular 348-cubic-inch V8, but it was standard with the 409. The Super Sport (SS) package consisted of special body and interior trim, power steering, and power brakes with sintered metallic linings, full wheel covers with a three-blade spinner, a passenger grab bar, a console for the floor shift, and a tachometer on the steering column. With the 409 engine, there was no alternative to the four-speed manual transmission and the factory supplied only one

axle ratio. Over the parts counter, though, it was possible to buy a pair of lower ratio gear sets to replace the standard set-up and obtain better acceleration. In regular trim, an Impala SS 409 would accelerate to 60mph in 7.8 seconds and turn quarter-miles at the strips in the high 15s. That took some beating in 1961.

The SS 409 could be made to go very well indeed on the street, but it was never very effective in formal competition. One problem was that the 409 engine did not lend itself to performance tuning: as in the 348 on which it was based, the wedge-shape of its combustion chambers was achieved by an angled head-to-block joint, which didn't permit increases in the compression ratio. As the 409 already came with an 11.25 compression and a four-barrel carburetor, there was little which could be done to it by traditional tuning methods.

Nor were the original Impala SS 409s very easy to come by. Production problems at Chevrolet ensured that no more than 142 were built in the 1961 season, and most of those became press demonstrators, went to favored Chevy customers, or wound up in the hands of professional drag racers who, Chevrolet managers thought, would gather the right sort of publicity for the division. Perhaps, though, that very rarity helped to fuel the legend of the 409.

The 409 didn't help Chevrolet to beat Ford in 1961, either on the NASCAR ovals or in the sales race. But it did give the division an edge on the streets and at the drive-ins, where the opinions which would influence more and more car sales in the coming years were being formed.

1962

A Little Competition

If 1961 had seen the run-up to the Muscle Car era with the arrival of Chevrolet's potent 409, it was 1962 which reflected that car's impact on the market when Ford and Chrysler both pitched in to follow Chevrolet's lead. But there were still very few Muscle Cars around (at this stage that description hadn't yet been invented for them), and the new breed of high-performance engines still belonged firmly within the full-size sedans where high-performance engines had always belonged. The signs of change are apparent now, but they were less so then. When Chrysler put its new high-performance big-block engine into its newly downsized Dodges and Plymouths, it was unaware that these cars presaged the Muscle Car proper, with its big engine in the body of an intermediate sedan. Some of 1962's high-performance cars were too highly strung to be useable on the street, but that, too, would change in time.

Another important factor at this time was that the National Hot Rod Association changed its rules for 1962, insisting that engine and body parts for its stock drag racing classes had to be production options which were actually available to ordinary customers through the showrooms. This would have even more effect later on, but for the new season it meant that the first thinly-disguised drag racers appeared on manufacturers' options lists right across America.

The 409

Chevrolet soon recovered from the production problems which had limited the availability of their 409 in the first months of 1961, and made a determined effort to exploit the engine to the full for the 1962 season. So, for its first full season of production, the 409 became available in all the full-size Chevrolets – Biscaynes and Bel Airs as well as Impalas. It was probably a good thing it did, because the new roof styling on the 1962 Impala hardtops made these less slippery than the '61s had been, with the result that the racers were discouraged from buying them. Instead, they turned to the Bel Air coupé, which still had a more aerodynamic slantback shape and had the additional advantage of being markedly lighter than the Impala.

Even though the 409 did not lend itself easily to performance tuning, the Chevrolet engineers had managed to squeeze more power out of their star performer by fitting new cylinder heads and a revised camshaft. In standard trim, with a single four-barrel carburetor, the 1962 409 delivered 380bhp; but it could also be had with a pair of Carter AFB four-barrels and a lightweight valvetrain, in which guise it thundered out 409bhp. One brake horsepower per cubic inch was really something to shout about in mid-1961, when this option was announced, and it was not at all surprising that the legend of the 409 went on to an even greater currency than it had enjoyed with the 1961 Impala SS 409s.

Other manufacturers must have howled in fury when Chevrolet's hot V8 attracted some very welcome and powerful free publicity through the medium of a pop song. The legend of the 409 had caught the imagination of Brian Wilson, leader and songwriter of the Beach Boys, and in mid-1962 he got together with lyric writer Gary Usher to create "409," a song which neatly pictured a typical California teenager dreaming of the time when he could buy his very own big-block Chevy muscle machine. After that song hit the streets, there can't have been many who still called the engine by its proper Chevrolet name of Turbo-Fire V8!

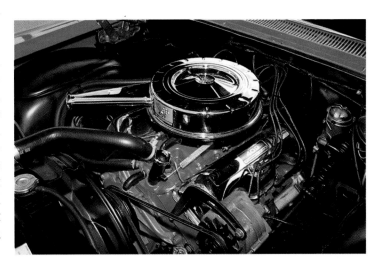

LEFT: Chevy's 409 became more widely available for 1962. This gorgeous ragtop is an Impala SS 409, complete with the SS trim package. Meanwhile, under the hood, the 409-cubic-inch motor (ABOVE) thundered out 380bhp in stock trim or one horsepower per cubic inch when fully optioned.

But for 1962, the 409 no longer had things all its own way. There was serious competition from Chrysler Corporation's new downsized Dodges and Plymouths, and Chevrolet were forced to take steps to redress the balance. Toward the end of the 1962 season, they introduced a set of aluminum front end panels for the Bel Air models which knocked 130lb off the cars' weight. These aluminum panels were available over the parts counter as replacement items for stock panels, or could be had as original equipment on special factory-assembled lightweight cars built in small numbers only. It was one of these lightweight Competition Specials, a Bel Air

Sport Coupé with a 409bhp engine, which turned in a 12.83-second quarter-mile during 1962. Cars without the lightweight panels were of course not *that* fast, but sub-15-second quarter-miles and 0-60mph standing starts of 6.3 seconds were quite enough to ensure the Bel Air 409s a special place in the affections of the street-racer crowd.

The big Fords

Like Chevrolet, Ford entered the 1962 season with something of a reputation. At the close of the 1961 season, they had uprated their 390-cubic-inch V8 to produce 401bhp, which gave the big Galaxies a street performance to be reckoned with and represented a direct threat to the Chevrolet 409. For 1962, they aimed to do better, and the high-performance news from Dearborn at the beginning of the season was that Ford would be fielding a 406-cubic-inch motor.

The big-block V8 had started life in 1958 as a 332, had rapidly been enlarged to a 352, and then in 1961 had become the 390. In 1962 406 form, it came in two variants, with a single four-barrel Holley carburetor and 385bhp, or with the Super High-Performance Tri-Power option of three Holley dual-barrels, and 405bhp. With just under one bhp per cubic inch, Ford found themselves unable to counter Chevrolet's proud boast about their 409, and it was partly for this reason that the 406 was almost hidden in the Ford options catalogues.

Unfortunately, Ford had something of a problem at this time. Although they had a fine new muscle motor, they did not have a car which could make the most of it. The 406 went into the big and heavy full-size Galaxies, and later into the Galaxie 500 and 500XL when these were introduced in mid-season. Although the Galaxies did give a good account of themselves in the NASCAR 500-mile races (after which the 500 and 500XL models were named), they were less impressive on the strip. A 405bhp Galaxie could accelerate hard to 60mph, but after that its weight and poor aerodynamics started to count against it, and cars in stock trim ran quarter-miles in the high 15s. This was not the stuff of which legends were made.

Ford rapidly reached the conclusion that it was the Galaxie's poor aerodynamics which were preventing it from attaining greater success in NASCAR events. The restyled roofline of the 1962 models created more drag than that of the 1961 cars, and Ford tried hard to remedy this. First, they announced a "Starlift" detachable hardtop for the Galaxie Sunliner convertible, which gave the car a roofline very similar to that of the 1961 Starliner. However, NASCAR refused to accept Ford's argument that this was a regular production option and would not allow the Galaxies to race with it. Then Ford announced optional extras in the shape of weight-saving aluminum bumpers and fiberglass body panels for the Galaxies, but again

NASCAR refused to accept that these were available in sufficient quantities to qualify as regular production items. As a result, the lightened Galaxies had to run in the Factory Experimental class, which did not produce the publicity bonus Ford had hoped for from success in Super Stock events.

The 1962 Galaxie with the 406 motor was therefore rather a disappointment to Ford, who were keen to secure a strong position in the high-performance market as it began to open up at the beginning of the 1960s. Yet the car was a clear statement of intent, and it also made it quite plain that the Ford engineers knew what they were doing. The 406 came as a package with four on the floor, any one of a series of optional low-ratio axles, 15-inch-diameter wheels instead of the 14-inchers fitted to regular Galaxies, fade-resistant drum brakes, and a collection of heavy-duty suspension components. Trim options also demonstrated that Ford had understood the market: already the top-flight Galaxie 500XL hardtop had the bucket seats and center console which became so important in the high-performance car market. In 1962, Ford certainly did not fail through want of trying.

Chrysler's Max Wedge

Whie it was predictable that Chevrolet would continue with the 409 for 1962, and that Ford would attempt to steal some of its thunder, few people can have expected

The convertible body on Ford's Galaxie for 1962 (LEFT) was more for the street and the drive-in than the weekend drags, but it could still be had with the potent 406 motor, pictured here on the right. This FE-series V8 has the full-house Super High-Performance Tri-Power option of three dual-barrel Holley carburetors and was good for 405bhp. The gold-painted valve covers are stamped with the Thunderbird name, although the 406 wasn't available in the Thunderbird itself.

the blockbuster with which Chrysler entered the high-peformance world that year. That blockbuster was the 413-cubic-inch engine which enthusiasts came to call the "Max Wedge."

In fact, the 413 didn't appear until the spring of 1962, and it wasn't *all* new even then. The basic motor with its wedge-shaped combustion chambers had been around since mid-1958, when it had been announced as the powerplant for Chrysler's New Yorker and Imperial ranges. For 1959, the 413 had boasted just 350bhp (or 380bhp in the performance-model Chrysler 300E), and a lot of that power had been used up in just getting these 4500-5000lb automobiles moving at respectable speeds. 400bhp came up for 1960 and 1961, but the engine was still available only in large and heavy sedans, and even the Chrysler 300F and 300G no longer had any pretensions to high performance. From the spring of 1962, however, the 413 came in certain models with an advertised 410-420bhp, which some experts claim was in reality very much nearer 500bhp.

How had Chrysler achieved this transformation? The first change the company's engineers had made was to open out the inlet and exhaust ports to take larger valves than came with the regular 413 (which remained available in the large sedans). The second was to add dual four-barrel Carter AFB carburetors on a short-ram inlet manifold. In this arrangement, each carburetor was located at

the end of inlet tracts which fed the cylinders on the opposite side of the engine. As the fuel/air mixture passed from the carburetor through these tracts, it gathered speed and was "rammed" into the combustion chambers, boosting power in much the same way as a supercharger or turbocharger does. This ram-induction had been seen on earlier Chryslers, when it had been blessed with the name of SonoRamic.

Yet the real stroke of genius did not lie so much in what Chrysler had done to the engine as in their choice of the cars to carry it. Here was a brutally powerful big-block motor, and instead of dropping it into a 4500-5000lb sedan, Chrysler chose to put it into a pair of sub-3300lb automobiles. The effect was staggering.

The sedans which received the 413 were the Dodge Dart (and its plusher Polara variant) and the Plymouth Belvedere. The bodyshell which they shared had been downsized for 1962, and sat on a 116-inch wheelbase – 3 inches shorter than was then the norm for the large sedans they pretended to be. Chrysler had guessed that, in a market which was now turning to the new compacts, the full-size sedans should also become smaller – but they had been wrong. Worse, the 1962 Dodges and Plymouths were saddled with some of the ugliest styling ever seen on an American sedan. These two factors caused sales to take a nose-dive. By the spring of 1962, therefore, the Dodges and Plymouths were very much in

need of the shot in the arm which Chrysler hoped the 413 would provide.

It wasn't easy to cram the 413 into the engine bays of these cars, and the Chrysler engineers had to develop a set of exhaust headers which curled up and then back in a ram's horn sweep. The installation was essentially the same in both Dodge and Plymouth models, and the engines had identical specifications – although Dodge called theirs by the evocative name of Ramcharger while Plymouth settled for the more descriptive Super Stock 413 title. Three-speed floor shifts were standard, and the Dodge models could be ordered with a pushbutton three-speed Torqueflite automatic box.

The 413 was definitely not a street motor, and in fact Chrysler advertised it as for competition use only. As a result, most 413s found their way into stripped-out two-door sedans. Plymouth produced a batch of special lightweight Super Stock models for competition, and most of the Ramcharger-equipped Dodges were low-specification Darts rather than Polaras. At the strips, the combination of the 413 with these lightweight sedans – lighter even than Chevy's Bel Air 409 – produced some shattering performances. The other makers of high-performance sedans could not but sit up and take notice.

The new motor did not save Dodge and Plymouth from embarrassing end-of-year sales figures for 1962, but it did give both marques a significant image boost. For 1963, Chrysler would be able to hold its head high alongside the high-performance market leaders.

Which cars really mattered?

Looking back at 1962, it is easy to get a distorted picture of the emerging muscle-car scene. NASCAR results, important in their own way but far less influential on the opinions of the street racers than quarter-mile times, show that the big-track events in 1962 were dominated by Pontiac with the Catalina, which racked up 22 wins. Chevrolet claimed just 14 victories, and Ford showed well with the Galaxies in 500-mile events.

For the young, high-performance car enthusiast in 1962, however, things looked radically different. Drag racing results were a far more accurate reflection of the way a car could be expected to perform at illegal races on the outskirts of town or at impromptu drags from the traffic lights on a Saturday night. What cut the ice with buyers like these was the fact that 409-powered Bel Airs took the Super Stock and Stock Eliminator classes at the Nationals, won the Super Stock event at the Winternationals, and racked up a whole series of lesser drag-racing successes in between. The absence of the Dodge and Plymouth 413s from NASCAR honors lists was of no importance compared to the fact that 413 Ramchargers set no fewer than four NHRA class records in 1962 and won that year's NHRA Championship. Nor did it count when performance-car fans knew that it was a 413-powered Plymouth which in July 1962 had become the first stock passenger car to run the quarter-mile in under 12 seconds. In this kind of company, the big Fords and Pontiacs were simply also-rans.

The big Pontiac Catalina (ABOVE LEFT) with its 421-cubic-inch motor dominated NASCAR events in 1962, but the market was already turning away from cars like this. The season's real performance hit was the Dodge Dart 413 (ABOVE), and its companion, the Plymouth Belvedere. The Dart was an ugly-looking sedan with a brutally powerful V8 which made it into a dragstrip stormer. Few customers bought one for street use, as the power and torque delivery of the Ramcharger motor made it almost impossible to drive in traffic. The carburetors (RIGHT) were located at opposite sides of the engine, at the ends of ram-induction intake manifolds.

Muscle Car Choice – 1962

Chevrolet Bel Air SS 409
Dodge Dart 413
Ford Galaxie 500XL
(with 406 option)
Plymouth Belvedere
(with 413 option)

1963

The Regulations Game

Concerned at the way the horsepower race was hotting up, NASCAR, NHRA, and other authorizing bodies agreed to impose a limit on engine sizes for the 1963 season. That limit was set to European capacity standards at 7 liters, which translated as 427 cubic inches, and its impact was immediately felt on the 1963 new-model announcements. Ford's new high-performance motor bore the 427 name, even though its actual displacement was only 425 cubic inches, and the new big-block V8 in Dodges and Plymouths was a 426. At mid-year, Chevrolet announced a 427 development of the 409, although few were made because GM instructed all divisions to pull out of racing in February 1963. Factory-backed Chevies and Pontiacs disappeared from the tracks overnight, although privateers continued to campaign hot Impalas and Catalinas with some success.

There were other developments in the high-performance world for '63. The trend toward lightweight panels for competition use which had been seen during the '62 season now spread, and during '63 lightweight modifications became an accepted feature of the competition scene. At the other end of the scale, manufacturers had realized that the hot Super Stocks were sometimes ill-suited to everyday street use, and so they made automatic transmissions optional on several '63 models as a way of ensuring wider sales than four-on-the-floor models alone were likely to achieve.

Pontiac – the big 421

Pontiac had been doing well on the NASCAR ovals, but their cars were too big and too heavy to take honors at the dragstrips – a problem which the division determined to remedy as soon as possible. The 1963 models were only slightly lighter than the '62 cars, but their new and sharper styling was carefully calculated to appeal to younger buyers, and prepared the ground for what Pontiac had in mind for '64.

For 1963, Pontiac also put two new high-performance motors onto the market. Both were based on the existing and well-respected 421, which had been in service since the beginning of the 1961 season and had already powered the big Pontiacs to success at the Daytona 500 races. The 421s were offered for the first time in all the full-size Pontiacs as alternatives to the regular 389, but

favorites with high-performance enthusiasts were the two-door Catalinas, which were the lightest and cheapest models in the full-size range.

The less powerful of the new 421s was the Trophy 421 HO (High Output), which mustered 370bhp at 5200rpm with triple Rochester two-barrel carburetors operated by a progressive throttle linkage. This Tri-Power 421 proved the popular choice, offering quarter-miles in the mid-14s when installed in the two-door Catalina and even giving owners of the 230lb-heavier Grand Prix hardtop quarter-mile times in the low 15s. That sort of performance from a full-size model straight off the showroom floor gave the 1963 Pontiacs a new credibility with performance enthusiasts, who could order their 421s with three-speed or four-speed manual gearboxes or with a Super Hydra-Matic self-shifter.

The Tri-Power 421 was the street motor; for serious strip or track use, buyers could specify the Super Duty 421, which came in three states of tune. The mildest of these had 390bhp and breathed through a single four-barrel carburetor; next up was a 405bhp version with dual four-barrels; and right at the top came a 410bhp type with the dual four-barrels allied to a high compression ratio. Only 88 of these special-order motors were built, and 11 of those went into some very special Tempest compacts for strip use. Catalinas with this top-line option could run the quarter-mile in under 14 seconds, and accelerated to 60mph from a standing start in 5.4 seconds.

Pontiac were well aware that weight was still likely to hold them back at the drags, and resolved to slim the Catalina down to make it competitive with the smaller and lighter Dodges and Plymouths. So the factory built a limited number of Super Stock lightweight Catalinas with lightened frames, aluminum axle centers, aluminum front panels and front and rear bumpers, plus a whole host of other modifications. These formidable machines, 300lb lighter than the lightest '62 Catalinas and powered by the Super Duty 421, could turn in quarter-mile times in the low 12s with a terminal speed of more than 116mph. Sadly for performance enthusiasts, not many had been made before GM instituted their complete ban on competition activity, forcing Pontiac to stop building them.

This red 1963 Chevy Impala hardtop looks relatively innocent . . . but a look under the hood shows that it was in fact one of the very rare models with the 430bhp Z-11 427 motor. This couldn't be had through the showrooms in the regular way, but was only available to factory-approved customers and was specifically designed to give Chevrolet a dragstrip winner. Sadly, GM pulled its division out of competition before the 427 could make its mark.

Half a season with Chevrolet

Riding high on their 1962 trouncing of Ford in the sales stakes, Chevrolet could do no wrong for 1963. The division finished the year as top dog once again, outselling Ford by an even bigger margin. Some of that sales increase was undoubtedly the result of the high-performance image which the 409 motor had created, an image which lingered on even after Chevrolet were obliged by the GM ban to withdraw from involvement in racing in February 1963.

Like the other Muscle Car manufacturers, Chevrolet had come to recognize by the end of the 1962 season that more cars could be sold on the back of the high-performance models' image if only they could be made more suitable for everyday use. For 1963, they successfully broadened the appeal of the 409-engined cars by doing just that, and 1963 was to prove a record year for the 409. Nearly 17,000 of them found buyers during the season. As the Bel Air hardtop was no longer available, buyer preference switched back to the Impala.

Making the 409 more suitable for everyday use meant taming it a little to make it more tractable, and for 1963 Chevrolet offered a detuned version which had none of the temperament of its more powerful brothers. To enhance its appeal to those who were more concerned with what owning a 409 did for their image than with what it could do on the strip, they made a Powerglide automatic transmission optional with this motor.

Yet the detuned 409 did not compromise the engine's legend in any way. With 340bhp, it may have been lacking in ultimate performance, but its 430lbf ft of torque at 3200rpm were more than the original 1961 409 could boast, and in the lighter 1963 cars the engine gave quarter-miles in the high 15s and 0-60 acceleration in 6.6 seconds – more than enough to put many rivals to shame on the street if not on the strip.

For the serious performance enthusiast, Chevrolet offered the 409 with a single four-barrel carburetor and solid lifters in place of the hydraulic type in the detuned motor, and this version of the engine was good for 400bhp. At the top of the performance ladder stood a 425bhp solid-lifter 409 with two four-barrel carburetors.

Aiming all the time to go one better, and in particular to go one better than Ford, the Chevrolet engineers came up with a new high-performance engine in mid-season. Although it had been developed from the 409, the new 427 was actually a very different engine, with a smaller bore and a longer stroke. It was known as the Z-11 engine, and its most interesting feature was its angled valves, which gave it the nickname of the "porcupine-head" motor.

Few people ever got close enough to a Chevrolet 427 in 1963 to see the porcupine's spikes, though. The motor was made available only to factory-approved customers, even though it was on Chevrolet's RPO (Regular Production Option) list. It was usually found in Impalas with the factory-fitted lightweight front end – aluminum panels and bumper – and it offered tremendous performance. Although the advertised brake horsepower was no more than 430, a Z-11 in an Impala hardtop would walk all over the hot Fords, Dodges, and Plymouths on strip or track.

Unfortunately, the 427's career was short-lived. It had hardly been announced when Chevrolet withdrew from competition and stopped production. Not enough had been made for the engine to qualify for the Super Stock class in which Chevrolet had intended it to be run, which meant that those who had bought one were obliged to run their cars in other classes. As the engine was untried, they also encountered some problems, only to find that the factory was unable to offer advice because of the GM ban. It was a most unfortunate situation; but the 427 did come back, after a gap of three years.

Plymouth improved on their formidable 413 with 1963's 426, which powered a number of successful drag racers. The car (LEFT) sports a paint job and graphics typical of the strips, while the picture at top right shows a Ramcharger 426 in action inside a Dodge Polara.

BELOW RIGHT: the 1963 Chevy Nova wasn't yet a Muscle Car . . . but it would be made into one before long.

Dodges and Plymouths

For 1963 Dodge rectified their terrible mistake with the downsized '62 Darts. The Dart name was now applied to a proper compact model, and the full-size sedans grew once again to rejoin the class norm of a 119-inch wheelbase. Inevitably, they put on weight, and this meant that power would have to be increased considerably if Dodges were to remain competitive in the performance game.

The engine Dodge came up with for the '63 season was one they described as "the hottest performing power plant to come off a production line." Marketed as the Ramcharger 426, it was a bored-out development of the lusty 413, featuring enlarged inlet and exhaust ports, a heavy-duty valvetrain with solid lifters, and a strengthened crankshaft and con-rods with lightweight pistons in forged aluminum. For good measure, there was also a large-bore exhaust system.

As first announced, the 426 had a pair of Carter AFB four-barrel carburetors on a short-ram manifold, and was rated (most experts say conservatively) at 415bhp, or 425bhp in high-compression form. A mid-season tweak gave it bigger carburetors, enlarged combustion chambers, and a revised camshaft, plus a set of more efficient Tri-Y exhaust headers. Quoted power figures remained unchanged, but there was no doubt that the revised engine was even more brutally powerful than the original 426.

Behind the 426, buyers could order either a close-ratio three-speed manual transmission or a heavy-duty version of the Torque-Flite automatic with push-button controls and late upshift settings. The standard Sure-Grip rear axle had a 3.91 ratio, but for maximum acceleration the factory would provide a low 4.89 set of gears. The hottest combinations would make a Dodge 330, 440, or Polara scorch through the trap at over 115mph in the mid-12s, and factory lightweight cars with aluminum front panels scored success after success in the Limited Production category during 1963.

Unfortunately, the 426 could be a temperamental and unreliable engine. It also had serious tractability problems at low speeds, and Dodge warned that it was not intended for street use. So the street racers mostly stayed with the 413 for 1963, which gave a more manageable 340bhp and ensured that a two-door Dodge was still a serious contender when the traffic lights turned green.

The Dodges scored in NHRA events, but it was 426-powered Plymouth Super Stocks which saw success on the NASCAR ovals. As fitted to Plymouths, the 426 motor was in the same state of tune as in the Dodges, and it went through the same mid-season upgrade. In principle, it was available to special order in all the full-size Plymouth sedans, but in practice the serious performance enthusiasts went for the Belvedere and Savoy, which retained the 116-inch wheelbases of the '62 cars and were therefore rather lighter than the Dodges. For racing, Plymouth dealers could supply a lightweight package, which trimmed the two-door models down to within a few pounds of the 3200lb minimum for the Super Stock class.

1963 was a good season for Ford's big Galaxies at NASCAR. This Galaxie 500 ragtop (BELOW LEFT) has the 390 V8 under its hood. Fords could also be had with the 352 V8 (RIGHT), but with just 220bhp it was nobody's performance motor when the 406s put out 405bhp and the 427 delivered up to 425bhp.

With cars like these, Plymouths claimed 19 wins in the NASCAR Grand National series during '63, of which 14 went to driver Richard Petty.

Ford's late-entry 427

After the fiasco of 1962, when Ford found themselves without any really competitive NASCAR entrants, the company bounced back with a vengeance for 1963. The big Galaxies took 23 Grand National wins, securing first place in the series, and achieved a spectacular first five places at Daytona. On the NASCAR ovals, it was Ford's year, but at the strips no Ford won a major NHRA title.

There were two key elements in Ford's revival, which did not begin until February 1963 when the company made its mid-season introductions. For 1963½ (as Ford-speak had it), there was a sleek new Sports Roof body for the two-door Galaxie, which was two inches lower than the regular hardtop and offered just the right sort of aero-dynamic advantages needed for success on the super-speedways. Ford had clearly learned from their 1962 mistakes, and they backed up the Sports Roof with a potent new motor – the 427.

The Ford 427 didn't actually displace 427 cubic inches, but there was publicity advantage to be gained from having an engine of the maximum permitted competition size, and Ford needed every bit of help they could get to reverse Chevrolet's commanding sales lead. The 427 actually displaced 425 cubic inches, and was a big-bore development of the company's well-established 406. High revs came easily to this motor, thanks to a light-weight valvetrain with solid lifters, while bottom-end strength was taken care of by cross-bolted main bearing caps. With a single Holley carburetor, the Ford 427 gave 410bhp at 5600rpm, but the top performer had a pair of four-barrel Holleys and put out 425bhp at a high 6000rpm. Like Chevrolet, Ford dressed their high-performance motors with chrome valve covers, hoping that these would add to the engines' street appeal.

Both versions of the 427 came with a four-speed manual transmission, and no alternatives were available. Both also came with a performance package which consisted of heavy-duty suspension, axles, and brakes, together with uprated driveshafts and universal joints. As in previous years, the high-performance Galaxies had 15-inch wheels instead of the 14-inch variety that were standard on the regular models.

But the '63 Galaxies were still big and heavy cars, sitting on a 119-inch wheelbase and weighing between 3500 and 4000lb. Once they had built up speed on the NASCAR ovals, their high-revving motors kept them ahead of the opposition, but at the drag strips they were still too heavy to outrun the 409 Chevrolets and the 413s and 426s from Chrysler. On the street, it was the same old story.

Ford tried hard to improve the Galaxies' sprinting abilities by building 50 very special Sports Roof models for competition. These had stripped-out cabins with ultra-lightweight bucket seats, together with aluminum transmission casings and bell-housings. Fiberglass was used for the bumpers, front fenders, and the "bubble" hood which was necessary to clear a special aluminum high-rise manifold. Some cars even had doors made of fiberglass. With a claimed 425bhp from their 427 engines, the best these Galaxie stormers achieved at the strips was a startling 12.07 second quarter-mile with a 118mph terminal speed. For such big cars, results like this were impressive; but on the streets the standard models were regularly out-dragged by the hot Chevies, Plymouths, and Dodges.

1964

The Youth Market Explosion

Nineteen sixty-four was the year when America really woke up to the demands of the youth market. These demands had been growing for some time; greater freedom and wealth for teenagers during the 1950s had set the scene and the arrival at car-buying age of unprecedented numbers of young Americans – the Baby Boomers – did the rest. The auto industry's marketing men had seen it all coming, and they were ready for it. For 1964, the major manufacturers targeted young buyers with a determination never seen before.

Growing trends at the beginning of the 1960s had shown the way ahead. What young people wanted in a car was not air conditioning or power-adjustable seats; what they wanted was performance and excitement. To a car-crazy teenager in 1964, the ultimate status symbol was a sporty-looking model which would out-drag his friends' cars at the traffic lights. What sold cars in the youth market was therefore 0-60mph times and dragstrip successes; winning on the NASCAR ovals at average speeds no stock model could ever achieve was altogether less important in this market. So the major manufacturers switched the emphasis of their factory-backed competition programs to events which demonstrated standing-start acceleration in preference to those which demonstrated high-speed prowess.

The compacts which had fought off the hordes of imported sedans in the early 1960s were also dying by 1964, and the trend was once again toward larger cars. All General Motors divisions abandoned their compact ranges for '64, replacing them with larger models which fell into the intermediate size category. And when Pontiac came up with the idea of dropping a big-block V8 into one of these new intermediates to give a cheap performance car, the whole face of 1960s motoring was changed.

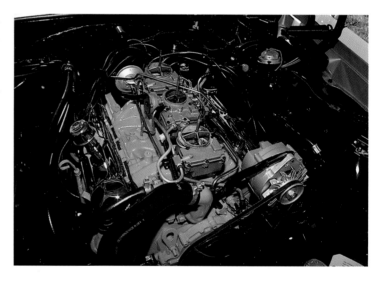

The 1964 Pontiac GTO introduced high performance at low cost in a package designed to appeal specifically to the emerging Youth Market. On the left is the lightest, cheapest, and fastest Sport Coupé; on the right, and overleaf, is the heaviest, slowest, and most expensive convertible. In the engine pictured above, the air cleaner has been removed to show the triple two-barrel carburetors which made up the 348bhp Tri-Power performance option.

The idea made a great deal of sense. Although the youth market was a relatively affluent one, its funds were obviously limited. Intermediates were by their very nature cheaper than the full-size models, and were therefore likely to sell to young people rather better. With less sheet metal to carry around, they were also lighter, and this gave them a performance advantage – as Dodge and Plymouth had demonstrated as early as 1962. As the NHRA/NASCAR ceiling of 427 cubic inches for competition engines still applied, the easiest way of getting more performance than could be had during 1963 was to fit the biggest permissible engines into smaller and lighter cars. And because young people wanted high performance for street use, no combination was likely to appeal to them more than a powerful, light, and cheap intermediate.

Pontiac's GTO – the car which many argue should be considered as the first real Muscle Car – was quickly followed up by imitators. Ford had considered that the best way to tackle the youth market was with a sporty compact which offered good rather than ultimate performance, and the success of the Mustang after its mid-season launch showed the company had not been wrong. But Dearborn recognised that it also had to compete with the newcomer from Pontiac, and rapidly cobbled together a special version of its intermediate Fairlane model for competition use. Oldsmobile also pulled out a GTO competitor very late in the season in the shape of its 4-4-2 model. Only Dodge and Plymouth, already scoring competition successes with the enormously powerful new Hemi Chargers, had no need to react to the threat from the GTO.

Pontiac – the mighty GTO

For '64, Pontiac continued to make the Catalina with its 421-cubic-inch motor. As in 1963, this offered up to 370bhp straight off the showroom floor with the Tri-Power option, and up to 410bhp in special-order Super Duty guise. The big Pontiacs were mildly facelifted and put on a small amount of weight for '64, but they still offered formidable performance for such large cars. It was sad that Pontiac were unable to gather more publicity with the Catalina because of the GM ban on factory competition activities.

But Pontiac did capitalize on the high-performance image the Catalinas had built up for them, and they did it with the GTO. The basis of the new model was the latest Tempest intermediate, which for 1964 used the new GM A-body shared by several other marques. Into that, the company had shoe-horned their big-block 389-cubic-inch motor, uprated with High-Output cylinder heads from the 421 and a high-lift camshift. In the light Tempest body, this gave performance even better than that of the bigger-engined but heavier Catalinas.

There are several conflicting stories about the GTO's origins. Some say that the idea came from Pontiac divisional chief John DeLorean, while others insist that the GTO was the brainchild of Jim Wagners, one of the company's advertising men, who enjoyed drag racing in his free time. Whichever is true, it is clear that some responsibility had to be taken at a high level because GM had actually forbidden its divisions to use engines larger than 330 cubic inches in the intermediate-body models. Pontiac found a way around the problem by offering the 389 big-block as an option, a solution which required no clearance from GM head office. Their aim was to sell 5000 Tempest Le Mans two-door sedans, hardtops, and convertibles with the GTO option. But the GTO was a runaway sucess. By the end of the '64 season, Pontiac had shipped more than 32,000 GTOs and had still been unable to keep up with demand!

What made the GTO so popular? Quite simply, it offered everything the street racer wanted at an affordable price. It didn't matter that Pontiac were unable to promote the GTO's virtues through a factory-sponsored competitions program, because the word about the car spread like wildfire. The GTO – soon to be nicknamed the "Goat" – could turn in sub-15-second quarter-miles at almost 100mph straight off the showroom floor, and with a 0-60 potential of 6.5 seconds it was a match for anything owners were likely to meet on the street, short of a full-blown dragstrip stormer. Add in all the stylish goodies of the time – bucket seats, console, floor shift and chromed rocker covers – and at its price the GTO was unbeatable.

The GTO package option put around 10 percent on to the cost of a basic Tempest Le Mans, but there were of course extra-cost options as well. The regular GTO package consisted of the 389 motor with a single four-barrel Carter AFB carburetor and 325bhp, a Hurst three-speed transmission, dual exhausts, uprated suspension, and quick-ratio steering. Even more performance was available with the 348bhp Tri-Power option of triple two-barrel carburetors, and there were regular and close-ratio four-speed manual gearboxes, or a Turbo-Hydramatic autobox which had been re-programed to suit the GTO's character. Axle ratios ranged from street cruiser down to low strip-stormer, a limited-slip Safe-T-Track differential and power-assisted steering were on the options list, and many buyers wisely specified the metallic brake linings which went some way to preventing the fade associated with the stock brakes.

The GTO name had been cheekily borrowed from Ferrari's formidable 1962 250 GTO for its connotations of high performance: the letters stood for *Gran Turismo Omologato*, which translated as "grand tourer homologated (approved) for racing." Not surprisingly, one specialist magazine took the bait and compared the fast Pontiac with the Italian sports-racer. It concluded that the Ferrari handled better and would therefore outrun the Pontiac over a road course, but that the Pontiac would prove the winner in a straight line contest. Moreover, it claimed, a Pontiac GTO fitted with the full NASCAR heavy-duty suspension would actually beat the Ferrari over a road course. True or not, that sort of conclusion fired the public imagination, not least because the Pontiac cost rather less than one-fifth as much as the Ferrari!

Teenagers drooled over the red GTO convertible on the preceding pages in 1964, but the 150-pound-lighter Sport Coupé pictured below was a tad faster and sold better. Neither, though, could match the shattering acceleration available from the Hemi-powered Dodges like that pictured right. For the moment, the Hemi was strictly a competition engine, but things would soon change as Young America demanded more and more street performance.

Like the Chevrolet 409 before it, the GTO inspired a popular song. "GTO" by Ronny and the Daytonas became a nationwide hit in August 1964, by which time the 1965-model GTOs had already been announced. However, recording dates and publicity pictures confirm that the subject of the song was the original 1964 car. And later, the GTO would go on to inspire several other drag-racing songs of the type popular before a new kind of music swept the nation in 1965-1966. The link between music aimed at the youth market and cars aimed at the youth market has rarely been clearer.

Chrysler – the Hemi returns

The MOPAR performance cars from Chrysler's Dodge and Plymouth divisions entered the 1964 season with the uprated version of the 426 wedge-head V8 which had been introduced mid-way through the 1963 season. This could be had in most of the full-size 119-inch-wheelbase Dodges, but serious racers knew that the lighter Plymouths – which all had the smaller 116-inch wheelbases – gave better performance. A 1964 Plymouth Belvedere with the 426 wedge-head motor was an extremely formidable challenger on the strip.

For the street, a detuned 365bhp version of the 426 Wedge gave vastly improved driveability in Dodges and Plymouths for 1964, and was quite fast enough for most owners: 6.8 seconds to 60mph was about par for a Plymouth Belvedere, although quarter-miles in the low 15s meant that cars like this were not competitive at national level. No matter: the competition versions of the 426 Wedge powered Dodges to top honors at the strips in the early part of the '64 season. But MOPAR wasn't content: it had one more trick up its sleeve for 1964. Just before the Daytona 500, at the beginning of February, Chrysler announced a brand new motor – the 426 Hemi.

Even the name sent a thrill of excitement through performance enthusiasts in 1964, for the Chrysler "Firepower" hemi-head V8 had been one of the key performance engines of the 1950s. The hemispherical combustion chambers which gave the engine its name allowed the fuel/air mixture to burn rapidly and also left room for huge inlet and exhaust valves, which improved gas-flow. In the new 426 Hemi – larger than any of the 1950s Hemis had been – the aluminum heads with their hemispherical combustion chambers were bolted to a reworked block from the 426 Wedge.

The results were shattering. Although MoPar adver-

tised the 426 Hemi with the same 425bhp as the 426 Wedge which it superseded for competition work, stories soon leaked out that the motor had nudged 600bhp on test. At Daytona, a Hemi-powered Dodge set a new record qualifying time for pole position. The factory-sponsored Dodges and Plymouths then scorched round the track at 175mph – 5mph more than any of their rivals could manage – and the Plymouths romped home to a 1-2-3 win. First-place driver Richard Petty later went on to win the 1964 Grand National title, a first for Plymouth, though Dodges took 14 first places overall as compared to Plymouth's 12.

Although Hemis were also formidable performers at the strips, they were not cataloged as regular production options and were therefore available only by special order. Serious customers could in theory buy one over the parts counter, or they could order a factory-built Super Stock model with the Hemi ("Super Commando" in Plymouth-speak) already installed. Dodge offered what they called a Maximum Performance Package on the 330/440/Polara-family cars, which teamed the new Hemi with a whole host of weight-saving options. These included aluminum hood, front fenders, doors, and other body panels, as well as a lightened front bumper, and magnesium front wheels.

This 1964 Dodge Polara 500 convertible probably didn't have the hottest of MOPAR's engines, which serious performance fans liked to put into the much lighter hardtop models. Sales, though, were undoubtedly boosted by the performance image which the hot models had created.

Ford at last produced a strip-stormer in the shape of the Fairlane 427, or Thunderbolt (BOTTOM LEFT), which dominated NHRA events that year. This one wasn't for the showrooms, however, and the Galaxie 500XL hardtop (LEFT AND RIGHT) was more typical of what street performance enthusiasts bought.

Stripped-out interiors ensured that these dragstrip-only cars were as light as it was possible to make them.

For the moment, the Hemi was not available to regular street racers, but who can say how much its reputation did for sales of the 426 Street Wedge, which remained available after the competition 426 Wedge had gone?

Ford strikes back – the Thunderbolt

At the beginning of the 1964 season, Ford had no news for performance fans. The big Galaxies were restyled, and the sleek fastback roof was carried over from '63, but under the hoods was the familiar 427. Yet no-one could argue that Ford didn't know what they were doing. The Galaxies were still too big and too heavy to be competitive except on the NASCAR ovals, but there they remained the cars to be beaten. During the early part of 1964 at least, a few rivals did beat them there, but Ford went on to set up a commanding lead which by the end of the season left them with a record 30 NASCAR victories and overall victory yet again.

In the sales battle with Chevrolet, Ford were counting heavily on their new Mustang, which they introduced at mid-year. And again they were not wrong – the Mustang was extremely successful. But for serious performance fans, there was nothing tempting about these first Mustangs. Ford recognized that fact, too, and when they decided to switch the main thrust of factory support from the NASCAR Galaxies to a drag-racing campaign which would attract younger buyers, they developed a very special new model. It was called the Thunderbolt.

Recognizing which way the wind was now blowing, Ford decided to follow Pontiac's lead by dropping a big-block motor into an intermediate sedan. Unfortunately, there could be no question of building a real GTO com-

petitor for the street just yet, because major production changes would have been necessary before Ford's Fairlane intermediate could accommodate anything larger than the 289-cubic-inch small-block V8. However, Ford reasoned that it would be financially viable to build a limited run of modified Fairlanes to mount an assault on the NHRA titles for 1964, and the remarkable Thunderbolt was the result.

The Thunderbolt was a hand-built car, which started out as a stock Fairlane two-door sedan. The front suspension and engine bay were then completely reworked to make room for the 427 motor with High-Riser inlet manifold and dual Holley four-barrel carburetors, exactly as used in the lightweight Galaxies. The cars were further lightened with a fiberglass bubble-hood (to clear the manifold) and plexiglass side windows; fiberglass front bumpers were also fitted at first, although later cars had aluminum ones. Stripped-out interiors were equipped with lightweight Police-specification bucket seats, and the back end was given extra weight from an oversize bus battery in the trunk, while anti-tramp bars on the rear suspension aided traction when all that power was put through the rear wheels. Transmissions were either a four-speed manual with an ultra-low axle ratio, or a Lincoln-derived automatic allied to even shorter overall gearing. Given the nature of these cars, it is hardly surprising that only 100 were ever built.

To get the Thunderbolts out to the drivers who would bring in maximum publicity, Ford sold a number to favored drivers (known as the Ford Drag Council) for $1 each. Joe Soap could also order a Thunderbolt through his local dealer for street use, but most cars went to the professionals for the very good reason that they were practically undriveable on the street.

The dragstrip-only Thunderbolt (ABOVE LEFT) was easy to recognize by its bubble-hood and twin air intakes in place of the inner headlamp pair. The air intakes led through massive trunking (LEFT) to force cool air into the induction system; under that air cleaner are two four-barrel Holleys.

The Chevrolet Impala hardtop pictured above right was a slick-looking machine, in this case equipped with nothing more potent than the 327, but the stance of the Chevelle Malibu SS (BELOW RIGHT) said everything about its performance pretensions.

Where it mattered on the strips, though, the Thunderbolt overwhelmed the longstanding dominance of the wedge-head Plymouths and Dodges. Thunderbolts regularly screamed through the traps at over 120mph to record quarter-mile times in the high 11s and low 12s, and by the end of the season they had managed to capture six of the seven NHRA division titles. For 1964, therefore, Ford's dominance of professional competition through the NHRA Thunderbolts and the NASCAR Galaxies was almost total.

Oldsmobile's late entry

Stung into action by the success of GM stablemates Pontiac, Oldsmobile realized that it needed to develop a street-performance intermediate in time to catch the tail end of the 1964 season. The car's late entry, combined with its less-than-stunning performance and rather confused image, hindered sales; but the concept was basically a good one, and was carried over into the 1965 model-year, when Oldsmobile did very much better in the Muscle Car market.

The Oldsmobile formula was similar to Pontiac's: take the lightest version of the intermediate sedan range and load it with performance extras. The intermediate sedan that Oldsmobile chose was the Cutlass, which actually shared a platform with the Tempest from which the GTO was derived, but Oldsmobile didn't have a big-block V8 to drop into their new Muscle Car. What they did instead was to make available through the showrooms Option BO-9 – the Police Apprehender Pursuit package with which they hoped to corner some of the high-speed chase/patrol car market.

What this meant was that the Cutlass' modestly powerful, 290bhp, 330-cubic-inch motor was given a four-barrel carburetor, a high-lift camshaft, heavy-duty rod and main bearings, and a dual-intake air cleaner. Dual exhausts were added; there was a four-speed manual transmission with floor shift; and the new model was given heavy-duty suspension with a stabilizer bar on the rear. Oldsmobile called it the 4-4-2 (four-barrel, four-speed, two exhausts). To add to the street appeal, the car was sold with bucket seats and a console as standard equipment.

The result of the engine changes was to put power up to 310bhp; torque remained unchanged, but the enhancement was enough to give the 4-4-2 the sort of performance which impressed on the street, if not on the strip. The 1964 4-4-2 could reach 60mph in 7.5 seconds, which was round about what the heavier, costlier, and more cumbersome Ford Galaxie with the 427 street motor could achieve. This was perhaps disappointing, but it did announce to the motoring world that Oldsmobile was back in the performance game after an absence of more than a decade.

. . . and where were Chevrolet?

Chevrolet had meanwhile also targeted the youth market for 1964 with their new Chevelle intermediate. Perhaps discouraged by the GM ban on competition activity, however, they seemed not to have thought of it as a high-performance model. Even when the division did manage to get a street-performance version into production and on the street in the middle of the 1964 season, they trailed far behind their GM stablemates Pontiac. The biggest problem was not even that the Chevelle SS arrived on the scene late; the biggest problem was that when it did finally arrive, it didn't really go.

Equipped with the small-block 327 motor breathing through a four-barrel carburetor, the Chevelle SS put 300bhp on the road. It was quick enough, but it had not yet reached the big league. Like its cousin the Oldsmobile 4-4-2, it was little more than a statement of intent.

Meanwhile, the faithful big-block 409 could still be had in the full-size Chevies for 1964. But the performance enthusiasts were already turning away from high-performance big cars, and production of the 409 motor dropped by 48 percent during 1964. Without factory backing, the big Chevies were also-rans in NASCAR and NHRA events that year. For 1965, Chevrolet would need more than a big-block now resting on its laurels and an underpowered intermediate aimed at the youth market.

Muscle Car Choice – 1964

Intermediates
Chevrolet Chevelle SS 327
Ford Thunderbolt 427
Oldsmobile 4-4-2
Plymouth Belvedere (with 426 Street Wedge or Hemi option)
Pontiac GTO

Full-size
Chevrolet Impala SS 409
Dodge Polara (with 426 Street Wedge or Hemi option)
Ford Galaxie 500XL (with 427 option)
Pontiac Catalina (with Super Duty 421 option)

1965

The Bandwagon Begins to Roll

As Detroit announced its new models for 1965, it became clear that the performance emphasis was now firmly on intermediate sedan models. Hot full-size models could still be had, but the real action lay elsewhere. Of the major manufacturers, only Ford had still failed to come up with a production intermediate (the Fairlane-derived Thunderbolt was a hand-built competition special). Instead, the Dearborn company had turned to high-performance versions of its new Mustang, which had been introduced mid-way through 1964 as a stylish but relatively tame sporting car.

The catalyst for this change of direction had been the Pontiac GTO. All of a sudden, every maker wanted a slice of the GTO market, not least among them those GM divisions which had not shared Pontiac's luck in finding a way around the 330 cubic inch ceiling for intermediate models. For 1965, GM was forced to raise that ceiling to 400 cubic inches – and its divisions responded with a range of new engines.

In professional competition, NASCAR tightened up its rules governing "production option" status in the wake of criticism that it should not have allowed Chrysler to use their special-production Hemi in intermediate Plymouths and in Dodges. The MoPar teams disputed this ruling and, as a result, did not compete for the first part of the season. This left the field open to Ford, whose storming Galaxies had their best-ever season, with 48 wins out of 55 starts.

Meanwhile, the NHRA had also introduced new rules. In the Super Stock class, cars now had to reach a minimum weight limit, which meant that the lightened front ends which had characterized the 1963 and 1964 cars became obsolete almost overnight. One result of this was that the F/X (Factory Experimental) class became more popular, as it allowed non-production high performance models which had been specially built by the automakers to demonstrate their prowess. This was fortunate for Ford, whose Galaxies were not doing well in the production class quarter-mile events, but who scored some notable successes with specially-equipped Mustangs in the F/X class.

On the street, the important options to have were bucket front seats (instead of a bench), a center console (usually tricked out with extra instruments or switches),

and a floor-shift (instead of column or push-button types) in automatic-transmission cars. Most high-performance pretenders offered some form of heavy-duty suspension, generally with anti-sway bars, extra location for the rear axle to prevent tramp under full torque, and a limited-slip differential. Other than that, the makers had already recognized the value of badging and trim details to make their high-performance models look different from the everyday models they were based on.

Exit 409, enter 396

For Chevrolet, 1965 was to be a year of transition. The venerable 409 remained available at the beginning of the season, but fewer than 3000 were built before it was replaced at mid-season by a new high-performance big-block engine. Meanwhile, the familiar 327 small-block motor saw out the season in a variety of different models.

The high-performance Chevies for 1965 were the Corvette – a sportscar rather than a true Muscle Car – the Chevelle SS, and the Nova SS. The old guard was still represented, however, and the high-performance engines also went into the restyled Impala and Caprice models, while some Biscaynes with the hottest of the available engines could demonstrate quite startling performance.

Smallest of the 1965 Chevrolet muscle sedans was the Nova SS, the top-line two-door hardtop model of the Chevy II compact range which sat on a 110-inch wheelbase. In price and intention, it was really a holding operation in the sporty-compact market, to allow the division to prepare its answer to the Ford Mustang. Smaller, lighter and cheaper than the industry-standard intermediates, it was an exceptional performer in its class. Fitted with the 300bhp 327-cubic-inch L-74 option (a 250bhp was also available), it wasn't quite up to the performance of the big-block intermediates, but it did have the right ingredients – a four-speed Muncie gearbox, for example, and a Positraction limited-slip differential.

Next up came the real intermediates, the Chevelles. Available with the 327 small-block since the middle of the previous season, these had detail revisions both inside and outside for 1965. For the first half of the season, the regular 250bhp and 300bhp options remained available, but in mid-season came something altogether more interesting – a 350bhp L-79 version. A Chevelle with the

ABOVE: For 1965, Pontiac gave their super-successful GTO the stacked headlamps from their bigger cars and came up with a car which was really good-looking as well as fast on the street. Sales soared.

RIGHT: This 1965 Chevrolet Impala SS is a real sleeper, as it looks quite ordinary but is actually equipped with the division's new 396-cubic-inch big-block motor. The engine was directly developed from the 1963 427 "porcupine-head" V8, which was Chevrolet's last new engine before GM banned factory participation in competition.

L-79 motor was one of the 1965's hottest streetable sedans, capable of turning in sub-15 second quarter-miles in standard trim. All came with four-speed manual transmissions and Positraction rear ends, which demonstrated that Chevrolet knew exactly what attracted the street crowd.

Chevrolet also knew how to keep the street crowd drooling, and at mid-season came a new and even more powerful engine option for the Chevelle. But the new 375bhp Chevelle was not made available through the showrooms. Just 201 were made, of which 200 were Malibu SS hardtops and one a convertible. All of them were supposed to go to Chevrolet officials, but it seems that a few did find their way into the hands of ordinary customers.

The engine which turned out those 375bhp was the new big-block replacement for the 409. Known as the TurboJet, or Mark IV big-block, this 396-cubic-inch motor was in fact not quite as new as it appeared. It was nothing less than a short-stroke, small-bore edition of the 1963 "porcupine-head" 427 Mark II big-block, the Z-11 competition option which had its life cut short when Chevrolet had withdrawn from competition. The changed dimensions had been forced upon the engine by the GM size ceiling of 400 cubic inches.

In the Malibu SS, the 396 was accompanied by a re-inforced frame (borrowed from the convertible models), heavy-duty suspension components, anti-sway bars front and rear, bigger brakes, and a quicker power-steering set-up. All the cars had Muncie four-speed transmissions, and in a straight line they could achieve some impressive figures. For the quarter-mile, a time of around 14.5 seconds and a trap speed of around 100mph were claimed. However, handling was another question altogether. The big-block motor made the cars very nose-heavy, which in turn gave them a tendency to plough straight on in bends taken at speed. Perhaps Chevrolet were right not to offer the Z-16 as a regular showroom option.

Nevertheless, the new 396-cubic-inch motor did become available off the showroom floor in the full-size models and in the Corvette. In the sedans, it came with 325bhp or 425bhp, the latter giving Biscayne drivers the opportunity to embarrass unsuspecting owners of quick intermediate models. And it proved enormously popular: in the 1965 half-season, Chevrolet shipped nearly 60,000 cars equipped with the 396 big-block. That figure is thrown into sharp relief when set against fewer than 44,000 of the legendary 409s sold in four seasons!

Oldsmobile, Pontiac – and Buick

It was Pontiac who had set the cat among the pigeons in 1964 with their GTO, and for 1965 they dished up more of the same. Like all GM divisions, they were still banned from competition, but that didn't stop them from offering cars which made good competition machines. The 1965

The Chevrolet 396 went into the Chevelle Malibu SS at mid-season, but was not a regular showroom option. Just 200 cars like this red hardtop were built (LEFT). The mighty Z-16 motor (BELOW) had 375bhp, which made the light Malibu very fast but endowed it with poor handling: note the brake servo, which was essential with the drum brakes Chevrolet still used.

On the street, the GTO (RIGHT) was still the best-selling Muscle Car, and most were fitted with the single four-barrel version of the 389 (BELOW RIGHT) which had 335bhp for 1965.

GTOs were restyled, taking on the stacked headlamps of the full-size Pontiacs, and they were equipped with a non-functional hood scoop. At least, it was non-functional on the regular models: for the lucky 200 or so customers who ordered the Ram Air dealer fitment option with the Tri-Power motor, that hood scoop was adapted to force air into the carburetor intakes for more performance.

Even the regular GTO models were quicker than last season's, however. The 389 motor with single four-barrel carburetor gained 10bhp to give 335bhp, and the Tri-Power option gained 12bhp to reach 360bhp, although it sacrificed a small amount of torque to do so. On the street, the GTO still held its own, and it remained *the* muscle machine to have, even though the competition from other makes was hotting up.

The full-size Catalina, meanwhile, was increasingly looking like a whale among the minnows. For 1965, it had actually increased in size as well as picking up new and more aggressive styling. Customers who wanted the car

to perform on the street chose the 421 engine, this year with 338bhp in single four-barrel form and 356bhp with Tri-Power. Right at the top came the 421 HO, with 376bhp and enormous torque to match, but the big Pontiacs were too heavy to hold their own with the best of the streetable intermediates.

Meanwhile, over at Oldsmobile, the division changed its strategy for 1965, and the 4-4-2 option was offered only on the lighter two-door models in the F-85, F-85 Deluxe, and Cutlass intermediate ranges. These all had trim and equipment changes to distinguish them from last year's models, but the most important of the 1965 novelties was under the hood, where the 4-4-2 now boasted a 400-cubic-inch motor in place of 1964's rather half-hearted 330.

That increase in size had been prompted by GM's new 400-cubic-inch ceiling for intermediate models, and Oldsmobile had created their new motor by reducing the bore size of the big 425-cubic-inch block which they used in their full-size models. With 345bhp, the intermediate

Oldsmobile could now boast respectable straight-line performance, but it was still not right up there with the leaders. If the customers were beginning to recognize that Oldsmobile did mean business, the warning issued with 1964's 4-4-2 had still not become an outright threat to other intermediates.

On the other hand, Buick's first entry to the Muscle-Car stakes demonstrated a lot more than good intentions. The Skylark Gran Sport, better known as the GS, was a mid-season arrival, making its bow in December 1964. Buick had created this GTO rival by taking their intermediate Skylark model, upgrading suspension and trim, and dropping in the nearest thing they had to a 400-cubic-inch engine. This was in fact the 401-cubic-inch motor first seen in the full-size Buicks for 1959, and known as the "nail-head" engine on account of its small, vertical valves.

At 401 cubic inches, the engine was strictly outside GM's guidelines for intermediate models, but the corporation no doubt recognized the likely cost of redeveloping the engine to lose just one cubic inch and therefore turned a blind eye. Even so, Buick promotional literature never referred to the engine in the Skylark GS as a 401: it was always either a 400 or else its capacity was not mentioned. One side effect of that ploy must have been that many customers did not recognize how old the engine really was!

With a single four-barrel carburetor and 325bhp, what Buick called the Wildcat 445 engine had less outright power than either the 389 in Pontiac's GTO or the 400 in Oldsmobile's 4-4-2, but it did have a great deal of low-down torque. With one of the optional low axle ratios, the Skylark GS could turn in some very quick standing-start times, although most of those sold were more for show than for go. Buick customers tended to specify luxury items, and the two-speed Super Turbine automatic transmission was more popular than the four-speed close-ratio manual which gave the best performance.

Like Chevrolet with their Chevelle-derived Malibu SS 396, Oldsmobile used the reinforced frame of their convertible models as the basis of the 4-4-2. To this they added heavy-duty suspension, fatter wheels and tires, plus, of course, the 401 motor and dual exhausts. To complete its appeal, the 4-4-2 had bucket seats, and it could be ordered with a center console and a rev counter as options. This, as Buick astutely recognized, was what impressed the street crowd almost as much as tire-smoking performance.

The 1965 Pontiac Catalina (BELOW) with its 421 engine was still quick, but it was too big and heavy to compete with the new breed of intermediate Muscle Cars like Buick's new Gran Sport (BELOW RIGHT). With a 401-cubic-inch motor which delivered plenty of low-down torque, the GS gave excellent standing-start acceleration. At the drags, though, cars like this Dodge Coronet Super Stock (RIGHT) with its special-order Hemi V8 were the ones to watch.

Dodge and Plymouth hang fire

Chrysler had a mixed year in 1965. NASCAR banned the Hemi engine from the intermediate classes, and the Super Stocks had to put on weight to meet the new NHRA regulations. Even so, Dodges did well in the quarter-mile events. Some cars also raced with fiberglass hoods and fenders in Factory Experimental classes and in events sponsored by other bodies.

Performance fans could still buy the formidable Hemi, which for 1965 was a special-order option in the Dodge Polara and in the new Dodge Coronet 500. The Coronet was a shortened and facelifted derivative of the 330/440/Polara series – down by two inches in the wheelbase to 117 inches and a lot prettier. In Hemi-powered form, it was sold as a two-door sedan, and Dodge also made it available with the 425bhp Ramcharger motor for strip use. Cars like these were not for street use, however, and Dodge catered for the street crowd by offering the Coronet with the 365bhp 426 Street Wedge. Not many were sold, though.

Dodge recovered from the dreadful styling of their 1962-1964 models
with the 1965 Coronet (ABOVE), available with a range of engine options
up to the 425bhp Hemi. Plymouth, meanwhile, found sales success with
their Satellite (BELOW), available with the 426 Street Wedge motor.

Over at Plymouth, the intermediate Belvedere range still carried the performance flag, although the image of the new Barracuda was undoubtedly causing that model to cream off some potential Belvedere sales. As yet, though, the Barracuda was not a serious performance car. The Belvedere Super Stock hardtop sat on a shortened 115-inch wheelbase and came with the 365bhp 426 Street Wedge (which Plymouth called the Commando V8) as standard, and the 425bhp Max Wedge for serious competition.

However, the best-selling performance intermediate from Plymouth was neither of these. Plymouth, too, had recognized the value of cosmetic goodies in selling their cars, and the Satellite hardtop and convertible – essentially a Belvedere sub-series on that model's 116-inch wheelbase – were tricked out with bucket seats and all the other street goodies. Entry-level Satellites had a 230bhp 318-cubic-inch V8, but serious performance *was* available, from the 426 Street Wedge.

The truth of the matter, though, was that the dispute with NASCAR had hit the MOPAR muscle models quite hard. Dodges and Plymouths returned to the NASCAR tracks late in the season, but it was too late to be of much consequence. Plymouth won four races, and Dodge won just two before the season ended.

. . . and Ford

Ford's big Galaxies were too heavy to shine in quarter-mile events, although they had their best-ever season on the NASCAR ovals, aided to some extent by the absence of Dodge and Plymouth. For 1965, though, Ford still had no intermediate performance model in production, and compensated by attacking the market in two different ways. On the one hand, they introduced some new high-performance derivatives of the hugely successful Mustang; and on the other they boosted their high-performance image with a stupendously powerful new engine which created its own legend.

The Galaxies were remodelled for 1965, with sharper styling creases and stacked headlamps, and underneath

they had a redesigned and tougher front suspension, while a new heavy-duty "nine-inch" differential could be ordered as an option. For the first half of the season, though, the big 427 motor remained broadly similar to its 1964 low-rise manifold equivalent.

It was mid-season when Ford introduced two new engines which made performance enthusiasts sit up and take notice. The less powerful of these was called the Thunderbird 427 Super High Performance V8, and was a development of the existing 427. Maximum power was unchanged, but competition durability had been improved by means of a large oil gallery low down on the left-hand side of the block which gave better lubrication. The so-called "side oiler" engine in the Galaxies was nevertheless quite overshadowed by another 427 development – the "cammer" engine.

The "cammer" 427 was in 1965, and probably remains today, the most powerful production car engine ever made. Ford had developed it with the express intention of taking on the Chrysler Hemis, and to that end their engineers had given the 427 block new heads with hemispherical combustion chambers. To cap that, they had fitted overhead camshafts – one per cylinder bank – and it was these which gave the engine its nickname. In regular single four-barrel form, the "cammer" 427 put out 616bhp, and with dual four-barrels it had a massive 657bhp.

With this kind of power, the "cammer" 427 was totally unsuitable for street use. This of course kept sales and therefore production volumes down, and NASCAR refused to accept the engine as a regular production option.

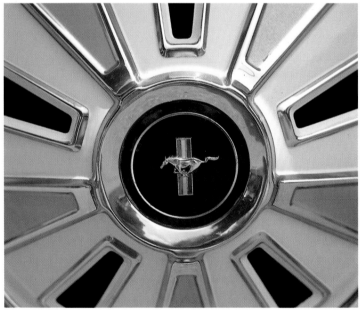

That nevertheless did not stop Ford from gaining maximum publicity with it in other events, both in the big Galaxies and in Factory Experimental Mustangs.

The original Mustangs, introduced in April 1964, had concentrated on style rather than on real performance. For 1965, however, Ford put this situation to rights. In came the Cobra 289 Hi-Po V8, first seen in the 1963 Fairlane, which pumped out 271bhp in stock tune and was packaged along with uprated suspension, fat tires, and all the recognized performance addenda. It gave the lightweight Mustang some commendably quick standing-start times for street use, although the car was not seriously competitive at quarter-mile events in this tune. Nevertheless, factory options (which remained rare) could pump output up as high as 343bhp.

However, the 289 Hi-Po Mustang was overshadowed after January 1965 by a new derivative. This was the work of Carroll Shelby, the former racing driver who had worked with Ford and with AC Cars in the U.K. to produce the legendary Cobra. Badged as a Shelby GT-350, the car was a Mustang fastback which Shelby had equipped with modifications to make it go, handle, and stop better. The 289-cubic-inch motor had a high-rise manifold and Tri-Y header pipes, and gave a lusty 306bhp in street tune. For competition use, Shelby offered the lightweight GT-350R, with around 360bhp. So extraordinary was *that* car that it took three class wins in its first race in February 1965, and went on to dominate and win the SCCA national B-production road-racing series.

Like so many of the most desirable high-performance cars, though, the GT-350 was never sold in large numbers. Just 562 were made during 1965, of which probably about 30 had the competition GT-350R specification. These Mustangs were not quarter-mile stars – Ford concentrated on Factory Experimental Mustangs for that – and nor were they NASCAR contenders. But for all that, they ranked among of the most coveted high-performance cars of their time.

Ford's Mustang ponycar looked better than it went in its 2+2 coupé form (LEFT), but became a serious Muscle Car when transformed by Carroll Shelby into the GT-350 (RIGHT).

Muscle Car Choice – 1965

Compacts
Chevrolet Nova SS 327

Ponycars
Ford Mustang 289 Hi-Po
Shelby Mustang GT-350

Intermediates
Buick Skylark GS
(with 401 option)
Chevrolet Malibu SS 396
Dodge Coronet 500
(with 426 Street Wedge,
426 Max Wedge,
or 426 Hemi option)
Oldsmobile 4-4-2
Plymouth Belvedere (with
426 Street Wedge option)
Plymouth Satellite (with
426 Street Wedge option)
Pontiac GTO

Full-size
Chevrolet Impala Caprice
(with 396 option)
Chevrolet Impala SS 409
Ford Galaxie 500XL
(with 427 option)
Pontiac Catalina
(with 421, 421 Tri-Power,
or 421 HO option)

1966

An Established Formula

No Muscle Car fan would think of 1966 as anything other than the year of the Street Hemi, the year when Chrysler turned their legendary race motor into a streetable powerplant and then took it back to the tracks to clean up in professional competition. But the hot Dodges and Plymouths were pretty much alone this year.

GM's ban on factory competitions activity remained in force, and so the battlefield was left to Chrysler and to Ford, who seemed to do everything wrong this year as far as muscle enthusiasts were concerned. NASCAR refused to accept their brutally powerful overhead-cam 427 as a production engine and, realizing that they hadn't a hope of competing against Chrysler's formidable Hemis with anything else, Ford withdrew from the superspeedways.

Ford didn't even get it right with the new hot intermediate which had been so long in coming. Making a late entry with it to NHRA events, they scored some successes but then failed to follow through with production on a respectable scale. And yet it was Ford who won the sales battle this year, finishing just ahead of Chevrolet with a

Still sleek and good-looking for 1966, and in this case equipped with the Street Hemi motor, was the Dodge Coronet (BELOW LEFT).

On the oval tracks, the new fastback Charger looked good and should have done well when running the Hemi (RIGHT), but it had airflow problems at high speed.

total production of 2.2 million. The enormous success of the Mustang was making clear that outright performance was not what sold motor cars. What the buyers wanted was a combination of usable performance and style.

Even so, the fastest cars were getting faster. The quickest of the '66 cars could turn in 14-second quarter-miles at well over 100mph straight off the showroom floor. Stopping them was a different ball game, however. American automakers had only just started to offer disk brakes as extra-cost options, and the old-fashioned drum brakes to which Detroit still clung with obstinate tenacity were simply not adequate for machines like these. It was also now glaringly obvious that the importance of strip competition had made Detroit's designers spend too much time developing cars which went very quickly in a straight line and not enough time developing suspension systems which would enable them to go around corners. The traction bars and anti-sway bars which were appearing on many of the Muscle Cars were little more than an attempt to shore up a crumbling edifice. The plain fact was that the handling of many of these high-performance models could be frightening.

Safety campaigner Ralph Nader and his cohorts had been drawing attention to shortcomings like these for some time, and in 1966 the safety lobby finally got its way. That year, the Federal Government announced new legislation which meant that all cars sold in the U.S. would soon have to meet a set of crash-safety criteria. In addition, they would have to pump fewer noxious gases into the air from their exhausts. The most powerful high-performance engines squandered fuel at an alarming rate, and were thus among the biggest offenders against the new clean-exhaust regulations. Clearly, this was going to

make a difference, and it certainly did begin to affect new-model plans.

In the showrooms, however, the GTO effect was still being felt. The best-selling muscle models were now intermediates, and interest in high-performance full-size models declined further. Galaxies, Impalas, and Catalinas all lost out to the new breed of hot intermediates. Yet Oldsmobile and Buick were still unable to emulate the success of stablemate Pontiac with the GTO.

Performance was filtering down to the sporty compacts, too, although the only really fast machine in this class was still the Shelby Mustang. But there were signs that others were aiming in the right direction, and it would only be one more year before cars like the Plymouth Barracuda could qualify as real high-performance models.

Chrysler – back with a vengeance

Chrysler had no intention of letting 1966 be as humiliating as 1965 had been. If NASCAR wanted to see a full-production engine before they would allow the MOPARs to race, then they would get one. For 1966, Chrysler stunned and delighted performance car fans by introducing an engine which some experts still believe was the best muscle-car engine of all time – the Street Hemi.

As that name suggested, the new motor was a streetable version of the legendary race Hemi, detuned to make it more tractable but still packing enough punch to give shattering performance to the cars it powered. Official figures rated it at 425bhp, but it certainly put out a great deal more. Expert estimates suggest that the real figure was somewhere between 500bhp and 550bhp, straight off the showroom floor. In most applications, the Street

Hemi offered 0-60mph standing-starts of less than 5.5 seconds, and sub-14 second quarter-miles with trap speeds of well over 100mph.

The Street Hemi did not put in its appearance until after the 1966 model-year had started, but it then became available in the Dodge Coronet and the restyled Plymouth Satellite. The lightest of the Dodges was the two-door pillared coupé, and this was the favored bodystyle for drag racers; but for street or combined street-and-strip use, the stylish two-door hardtop was an altogether more attractive option. The Plymouth came only as a two-door hardtop or convertible, which closely resembled the Dodge. Tractable though their engines were, however, these muscle machines were not for the faint-hearted. Braking was marginal (even with the enlarged Police-specification drums fitted as standard) and handling made only too obvious the fact that the main design priority had been to make these Dodges and Plymouths go fast in a straight line.

Dodge had one more trick up their sleeve for 1966, and they made the Street Hemi available in the Charger, a stylish new fastback model which arrived mid-season and was based on the 117-inch wheelbase Coronet. Most Charger customers settled for something considerably

less brutish than the Street Hemi, and in fact only 468 of the 1966 models – just over 1 percent of the total – had the 425bhp motor. But the Hemi Charger gave Dodge a formidable new contender in the very-high-performance market.

Hemi Chargers were capable of standing-start acceleration times similar to those of the Hemi-powered Coronets, but they showed up less well on the high-speed ovals. The Charger's problem was that its fastback body gave peculiar airflow characteristics which actually caused the back end to lift at speed. For this reason, later Chargers had a small rear spoiler which helped the airflow to force the rear end down on to the tarmac.

Plymouth's sporty fastback Barracuda was not offered with the Street Hemi during 1966, although that didn't stop privateers dropping Hemis into Barracuda shells to compete against the "cammer" Mustangs in the appropriate NHRA classes. Plymouth fans who wanted a Street Hemi from their local dealership had to settle for a Satellite, cleanly restyled along with the rest of the Belvedere series for 1966. Top motor at the beginning of the season was a 325bhp 383, but the Street Hemi showed up in Plymouths at the same time as it arrived in the Dodge showrooms. The Plymouth Satellite, one inch shorter in the

This 1966 Hemi Charger (BELOW) is one of just 4698 made that year, and its looks don't betray the powerhouse sitting under its hood. Headlamps were concealed behind dummy grilles to give a clean front-end look.

RIGHT: The legendary engine itself – its regular orange paint making a striking contrast to the red of the engine bay and firewall in this Charger.

wheelbase than Dodge's offerings, was also a little lighter, and could outrun the Dodges in the quarter-mile events on a good day.

Nevertheless, it was Dodge who cleaned up at NAS-CAR. Running once again with Hemis, Dodge drivers took the championship with a total of 18 wins. Plymouth, though, were anything but disgraced. With a total of 16 wins, they came second. It was a complete walkover for the MOPAR teams and – for 1966 at least – the name of Hemi was once again on every performance enthusiast's lips. On the street, where it mattered, Chrysler was the undisputed king.

Ford – sitting it out

Exactly what Ford thought they were doing in 1966 is anyone's guess, but there wasn't much doubt that they had chosen to watch the muscle-car scene from the side-lines. Perhaps they had simply been discouraged by the competition ban on the "cammer" 427 motor, or perhaps they were more concerned to sell the image of speed than speed itself. Certainly, that was very much the way it looked that season. They raced the "cammer" 427 in Factory Experimental classes to gather performance pub-licity; they kept their long-awaited new hot intermediate in the hands of the professionals; and they put their mar-keting effort behind lukewarm versions of the Mustang while taking the edge off the high-performance Shelby versions.

The publicity which the "cammer" 427 gathered did little good for anything except Ford's image. Enthusiasts were quick to recognize that the engine wasn't available in the real world, and for the street crowd this muscle motor might just as well not have existed. When they dis-

Plymouth offered an attractive range for 1966. New that year was the Barracuda (MAIN PICTURE), still gawky-looking and not yet available with real muscle through the showrooms. The Satellite ragtop (RIGHT) was a good-looking car, and was equipped in this case with the 325bhp 383 motor.

LEFT: The sleek, straight lines of the 1966 Dodge Charger.

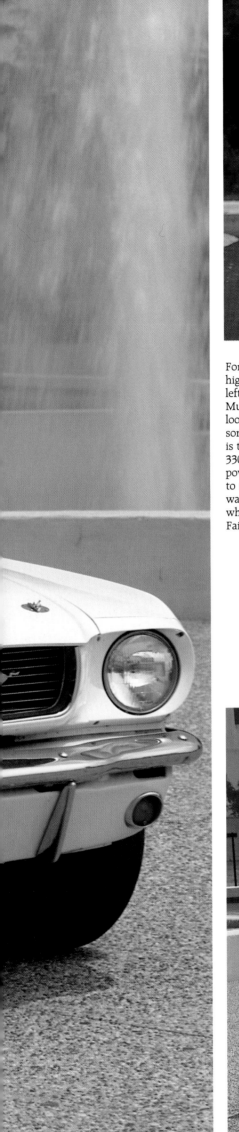

Ford didn't seem to believe in high-performance models for 1966: left and below is the Shelby Mustang GT-350, which still looked superb but had already lost some of its 1965 character. Above is the Fairlane GTA, which ran the 330bhp 390 V8 – the most powerful motor Ford was prepared to sell in quantity. The real action was reserved for professionals, who could buy a 427 powered Fairlane.

covered that the hottest of the new Fairlane intermediates which Dearborn was prepared to sell them was more about style than speed, many began to wonder just how serious Ford really were about high-performance motoring in 1966.

The new Fairlane could have done so much more for Ford than it was ever allowed to. In reskinnning their intermediate sedan for 1966 and revising its chassis, Ford made sure that there was enough room under the hood this time for a big-block motor: the Thunderbolt of 1964 had shown how effective such a combination could be on the strips. But Ford made two mistakes. First, they didn't announce the hot Fairlane until after the 1966 season had begun, and second, they didn't build the car in quantity. Only about 70 were made in the whole season, which suggests that the company was mainly interested in reaching the production level of 50 demanded by NHRA regulations and in going for publicity rather than sales. The street enthusiast was ignored.

The heart of the 1966 Shelby GT-350 was the 306bhp 289 V8, with valve covers bearing the "Cobra" name (LEFT). That same motor could be had in the GT-350H, specially produced for the Hertz hire car company and tricked out with a special paint job (BELOW RIGHT AND OVERLEAF). Many of these cars are said to have been used by their hirers for competition work at weekends.

The big Galaxies had definitely had their day, however. The new 428 motor fitted into the red hardtop (RIGHT) might have had more capacity than the redoubtable 427, but it was tuned for smooth torque rather than outright performance. Ford had recognized that the day of the full-sized Muscle Car was over.

Under the hood of the hot Fairlane was the 427 "side-oiler" motor with a single four-barrel Holley and 410bhp, or dual four-barrels and 425bhp at higher revs. Most of those made seem to have had the more powerful option. To fit the 427, Ford had to relocate the front suspension dampers, although the operation was nowhere near as costly as the major rebuild which had been necessary for the Thunderbolt two years earlier. A Special Handling Package was standard, and there was a fiberglass hood with a scoop which fed fresh air directly into the air cleaner.

With that combination, the 427 Fairlane certainly had performance. One professional estimate put the car's quarter-mile time in the mid-14s with a trap speed of 100mph. It wasn't the best of the 1966 intermediates, but it was up there with the front runners. Ford campaigned it in NHRA Super Stock events and did their high-performance image a lot of good in the process. On the street, though, it was hardly ever seen. Ford seemed to think they could keep performance fans happy by continuing to offer the Mustang with its High Performance 289 motor and the Shelby GT-350.

In fact, the Shelby Mustang wasn't the car it had been in 1965. Ford wanted to sell more for 1966, and the inevit-

able result was that the original race-ready car was toned down for greater acceptability. It still went quickly, but with far less of the sound and fury which had added to the 1965 models' appeal; and customers who insisted could now order it with a performance-sapping automatic transmission.

The Shelbys which did well in competition during 1966 were essentially last season's models. Carroll Shelby did his best to keep a high profile by persuading the Hertz rental firm to take a large fleet of the 1966 models (and these special-editions were known as the GT-350H) which it operated out of major airports. He also fought to retain the original high-performance nature of his machine by offering a Paxton supercharger as an extra, and this did put power up beyond 400bhp and bring the zero to 60 time below five seconds. Sadly, very few were built.

Even the Galaxies were no longer what they had been. Well aware that the big sedans had had their day, Ford replaced the top-line muscle 427 motor and fitted instead a 428 big-block, tuned for smoothness rather than power. With 345bhp, the Galaxie was nobody's performance car, and without the impetus of a factory-backed competitions program it did not sell well.

The 1966 Pontiac GTO came as a convertible coupé (RIGHT), as a sport coupé (BELOW) and as a hardtop coupé. The regular motor was the 389 V8 with 335bhp but, for extra cost, buyers could order the 360bhp Tri-Power 389. The 360bhp motor (LEFT) proudly shows off its three-carburetor power package, now in its final year because GM was about to ban multiple-carburetor set-ups for all divisions.

The General bides his time

Frankly, not a lot was going on at General Motors for 1966, either. However, the GM divisions already had some hot products on the market, like Chevrolet's 396 and the market-leading Pontiac GTO. This year was a time for building on their existing successes.

Nineteen sixty-six turned out to be the best-ever year for GTO sales, and the GTO sold more copies that year than any Muscle Car before or since. One reason for the increase in the model's popularity was undoubtedly its new styling, which introduced more rounded lines and a recessed rear window with stylish sail panels to the vertical-headlamp body of 1965. This and wider tracks made the car look bigger, too, although in fact the wheelbase remained unchanged at 115 inches. Detail trim apart, the GTO's new styling was identical to that of the Tempest – although this year the GTO was a model series for the first time rather than a Tempest option package.

Pontiac had no need to boost performance to attract more sales; they knew that the rivals from Buick and Oldsmobile could not offer GTO performance levels and were unlikely to in the near future. For 1966, the GTO therefore had exactly the same power options as for 1965: the 389 V8 came with 335bhp unless buyers chose the extra-cost Tri-Power package with 360bhp. A Tri-Power GTO would still make most of the competition look sick – although it couldn't keep up with a Hemi-powered Dodge or Plymouth – but 1966 was to be the last year of its availability. GM issued another one of its famous corporate bans at mid-year, which forbade all divisions to use multi-carburetor performance packages for 1967. No doubt there was a link between this and the forthcoming Federal exhaust

The 1966 Pontiac Catalina and the Chevrolet Chevelle SS 396 from the same year (BELOW RIGHT) show the two extremes of GM's Muscle Cars for that season. The Pontiac was a vast car with a 121-inch wheelbase, while the Chevelle sat on a 115-inch wheelbase and weighed some 750 pounds less. The Pontiac had a large but now elderly 421 V8 (LEFT) and was at its best with the Tri-Power performance package which would disappear under GM's corporate ban in 1967; the Chevelle had the latest 396 V8 (RIGHT), and was a match for Pontiac's GTO on the street.

emissions legislation – multiple carburetor set-ups must have been among the worst of the clean-air offenders – but it was a sad day for performance fans.

There was some compensation for the second half of the '66 season when Pontiac dealers offered a bolt-on performance package consisting of a hot camshaft and a kit to convert the dummy hood scoop into a functional fresh-air scoop. Some cars also seem to have come from the factory with these modifications. However, the package probably didn't make very much difference to performance; figures were never released, as they surely would have been if there had been something to boast about!

As far as the Catalina was concerned, however, the story reflected that same decline in interest which had been seen elsewhere in the full-size sedan market. Muscle models were no longer selling. For 1966, the big Pontiacs sat on the same wheelbase but had been restyled and were actually some 3 inches shorter overall. There was no saving in weight, however, and in fact the '66 Catalina was slightly heavier than the '65. Engine options were the same as before, with the 421 in 338bhp four-barrel form or 356bhp Tri-Power tune. The Catalina was still a swift mover, but fashion had now passed it by, and for 1967 it would pass out of the realms of muscle machinery as the venerable old 421 was withdrawn.

Over at Oldsmobile, the division's F-85 and related intermediate series went through a similar facelift to Pontiac's Tempest models. The 4-4-2 was marketed as a separate series this year, but it still shared the F-85's styling. That meant more rounded contours, with pronounced rear "hips," wider tracks and an overall larger appearance than on the '65 models. All the 4-4-2 range were two-door models, and all of them had GM's 1966 trademark recessed rear window with sleek sail panels

alongside. But they did not have a good year. Only 21,997 4-4-2 models found buyers in 1966, as compared to 28,500 the year before.

That was a shame, as the 400-cubic-inch motor had a raised compression ratio to give extra power and torque at slightly higher revolutions. The car certainly performed better than last year's, but it just wasn't in the big league. The lighter and cheaper GTO left it for dead at the strip and on the street, and even optional bucket seats and center console could not make up for the yawning gap between the two cars.

Even so, there were a few hotted-up '66 4-4-2s. Late in the model year came the L-69 option, with triple-two-barrel carburetors which boosted power by 10bhp to 350bhp. Published figures suggest that the torque was unaffected, but triple-carb 4-4-2s seem to have accelerated a lot faster than the stock models, so torque must have been greater. Not many were sold, and the option was deleted at the end of the year when GM's ban on multi-carburetor set-ups came into force.

Then for serious quarter-mile fans, Oldsmobile dealers could provide the W-30 package for the 4-4-2. This added a radical camshaft and ram induction, together with such goodies as a trunk-mounted battery (to improve weight on the rear wheels and therefore traction), fiberglass inner fenders at the front, and chromed engine parts (to look good when it wasn't moving). Just 54 of these drag-racing specials were put together during 1966 – not enough to make a serious difference to the 4-4-2's still rather lackluster reputation.

Chevrolet fielded a tempting line-up this year. The smallest of their performance models was the Nova SS, still on a 110-inch wheelbase and still based on the compact Chevy II sedan. The '66 restyle gave it rather more presence on the road, and performance options were also upgraded. Although the base-model SS had a lackluster in-line six, the muscle versions had the small-block 327 again, this time uprated to 275bhp and 350bhp. In its most powerful tune, the 327 would power a Nova SS to quarter-miles in the high 14s or low 15s, which made the car a credible budget street racer.

The Chevelle intermediate was also restyled for 1966, following the overall GM styling trend by becoming more rounded and looking larger than before. Dimensions were the same, though, as was the option of the 396 big-block V8 in the Malibu SS performance model. And this

year, it was a thunderous success. For 1965, just 201 SS 396 cars had escaped from the factory; this year, the SS 396 sold 72,300 copies in hardtop coupé or convertible form. Clearly, this was one of the things which Chevrolet had got right.

The base 396 offered 325bhp – rather less than the 350bhp from the small-block 327 V8 in the regular Malibu – but the L-34 option brought 360bhp and a dose of extra torque. Most '66 Malibu SS 396 models were delivered in one of these two states of tune, with three-speed, four-speed, or Powerglide automatic transmissions. The 360bhp version would out-drag a GTO to 60mph, although it was no match for the Pontiac over a full quarter-mile. On the street, though, these things mattered: drags from the traffic lights rarely lasted a full quarter-mile.

Right at the top of the performance options list for the Malibu SS 396 came the L-78, which was a 396 motor tuned to 375bhp. In essence, the L-78 was an updated version of the 1965 Z-16 motor. However, it was only sold in limited numbers, and there were probably no more than 100 made. Its 375bhp were more than the majority of Malibu SS 396 owners needed, which probably explains why the 425bhp Corvette version of the 396 motor never became available in these intermediates.

Full-size performance cars were becoming increasingly irrelevant by this time, but Chevrolet persevered with their hot Impalas. Sales of the Impala SS took a tumble, however, dropping by more than 50 percent as compared to 1965. The reason was twofold: performance buyers had

defected to the Malibu SS 396, and those who wanted the luxury of a large car were going for the luxury-edition Caprice.

At the beginning of the 1966 season, the big Chevrolets were available with the 325bhp 396 motor, but the big news came at mid-year. Chevrolet announced a new 427 big-block, a 396 bored out to the same dimensions as the 1963 "mystery" race engine on which it had been based. In street form and with hydraulic lifters, this offered a hefty 390bhp and a lot more low-down torque than the 396, which was enough to power a heavy Caprice hardtop to 60mph in less than eight seconds. The big Chevrolets could be made even faster with the optional "special performance" 425bhp version of the 427. To achieve the extra power, Chevrolet engineers had fitted a hot camshaft with solid lifters, and to ensure bottom-end durability they had gone for four-bolt mains. A new close-ratio four-speed manual transmission helped these cars to move very quickly indeed.

Even so, the big Chevies had few successes on the tracks during 1966. Without factory backing, privateers did what they could with the engine, and it was a 427-powered Biscayne which won Junior Stock Eliminator at the 1966 NHRA Winternational drag-racing championships. This was an exception, however.

Last for 1966, and trailing way behind the other GM divisions in the muscle-car arena, came Buick. The intermediate Skylark GS followed corporate dictates this year, becoming a series on its own instead of an option on the Skylark series, and its styling followed the rounded-contours and recessed-backlight pattern of the Oldsmobiles and Pontiacs. Power came once again from the 401 V8, which packed the same 325bhp until mid-year, when a 340bhp option became available. On the street, the hotter GS could stay with a GTO to 60mph, but once again the Pontiac was considerably faster over a full quarter-mile. The Buick remained unloved, though: sales were seriously down as compared to 1965.

Chevrolet's 396 V8 could be had in full-size models for 1966, such as the Impala SS 396 (BELOW). However, stablemates Oldsmobile had now woken up to the Muscle Car market, and for '66 offered an improved 400-cubic-inch V8 (ABOVE RIGHT) in their 4-4-2 model.

1967

The Peak Year

Many performance enthusiasts would argue that 1967 was the peak year for the American Muscle Car, and there is much to be said for their point of view. It was a year when a wider variety than ever of muscle machinery was available to mere mortals through their local showrooms, and it was a year when the increased competition in the marketplace obliged manufacturers to offer new and interesting options to keep ahead of the game and keep their credibility with the street and strip crowds. Nine-

teen sixty-seven was also the end of an era in some ways, however. For in 1968, new Federal regulations governing safety standards and exhaust emissions would force the Muscle Car to change.

Since the arrival of the Pontiac GTO for 1964, the trend had been away from full-size Muscle Cars, and 1967 took things a step further. Ford had already taken the Galaxies out of the arena; Pontiac now withdrew the big Catalina; and only Chevrolet bucked the trend, not only keeping

high-performance full-size models in their line-up but actually introducing a new model – the Impala SS 427 – during the course of the season.

The typical Muscle Car for 1967, therefore, remained an intermediate, with a wheelbase of 115 inches (Buick GS-400, Chevrolet Malibu SS 396, Oldsmobile 4-4-2, Pontiac GTO), 116 inches (Ford Fairlane 427, Mercury Comet Cyclone GT, Plymouth Belvedere GTX and Satellite), or 117 inches (Dodge Charger and Coronet R/T). But a growing new trend was also discernible. Following the success of the Mustang's high-performance derivatives, ponycars were appearing with muscle motors under their hoods. Chevrolet offered a pair of hot Camaros, including the legendary Z-28; Pontiac offered a 400-cubic-inch Firebird; and Plymouth leapt into the fray with the second-generation Barracuda.

By now, every serious street performance fan expected a center console, bucket front seats and four-on-the-floor, and so the automakers had to look for new options and gimmicks to sell their high-performance models. Disk front brakes, invariably with power assistance to counter higher pedal loads, were offered more widely than before. The racing stripes which had given the

Dodge was out in front again in 1967 with the 440 Magnum V8, an option in cars like this Coronet R/T 440 hardtop (LEFT). With 375bhp and a torque figure of 480 lbf ft at 3200rpm, it offered nearly as much performance as the legendary Hemi V8. The excellent torque spread made it very tractable for everyday street use, and the R/T 440 was certainly among the most enjoyable of the Muscle Cars to own. Meanwhile, Chevrolet had come up with a hot Camaro to counter Ford's muscle Mustangs, and the SS 396 (ABOVE LEFT) was a formidable machine indeed, even though its rear axle was not always well-behaved.

MOPAR muscle offerings for 1967 included the Plymouth Belvedere GTX (ABOVE), Plymouth's equivalent of the Dodge Coronet R/T 440. The Plymouth was rather lighter and faster than the Dodge, although it shared the same 440-cubic-inch motor, which was known in Plymouth-speak as a Super Commando V8. The car looked innocent enough in hardtop form; the motor (LEFT) didn't need a chrome dress-up kit to look as if it meant business.

The Dodge Charger (ABOVE RIGHT) was still discreet enough not to be instantly recognizable as a high-performance car. This one actually has a 426 Hemi under its hood.

Shelby Mustangs so much of their visual appeal as long ago as 1965 had spawned a new decorative art form, and decal stripes began to appear on other manufacturers' hot machinery. And GM, well aware that add-on tachometers were sometimes next to invisible and always looked untidy, tried a new gimmick with tachometers mounted in pods on the hood ahead of the driver.

Engines, on the whole, were getting larger. Pontiac went to 400 cubic inches for their 1967 GTO, Shelby Mustangs for '67 could be had with a 428 big-block, and the new hot motor in Dodges and Plymouths displaced 440 cubic inches. A lot of stock machinery could run quarter-miles in under 15 seconds, and the good news was that Detroit had finally learned how to make its fast cars tractable, and was rapidly coming to terms with the idea that they also needed to handle and stop well. The Muscle Car was getting more civilized, but it had not yet lost its teeth. . . .

On the superspeedways, it was MOPAR all the way for '67. Richard Petty earned his nickname of "The King" by taking 27 of Plymouth's 31 Grand National wins this year; stablemates Dodge by comparison achieved just five wins; and Ford hardly rated, although the publicity they made out of winning the Daytona 500 might have led potential customers to think otherwise!

Chrysler – still on top

For ultimate strip or street performance, muscle car fans in 1967 still needed to look no further than Chrysler's Dodge and Plymouth line-ups. The really serious performance enthusiast could still buy the legendary Hemi, installed either in Dodge's Hemi Charger – changed only in detail from its '66 incarnation – or Plymouth's Satellite Street Hemi and new Belvedere GTX. It was the Hemi which the MoPar teams still campaigned in NASCAR racing – and to devastating effect. All of Richard Petty's NASCAR wins were in Hemi-powered Belvederes, while the successful Dodges were Hemi Chargers. And for the strip, Plymouth offered stripped-out Super Stock Belvederes to special order, equipped of course with the 425bhp 426 Street Hemi.

The Hemi was largely for professionals, though, in spite of its new-found (for 1966) tractability. For 1967, Chrysler's masterstroke was to bring near-Hemi performance to the street in cars which were as usable as any customer could wish for. They did it with a new big-block motor, which was called the 440 Magnum in Dodge guise and the Super Commando V8 when fitted to a Plymouth model.

In fact, the new 440-cubic-inch V8 was only new to the intermediates. For 1966, it had been available in the full-

The '67 Dodge Coronet had a 117-inch wheelbase and was no lightweight, but it had considerable appeal to performance fans. Both the blue convertible below, and the cream hardtop on the left, pack 426 Hemi power under their hoods, although for street use there was little doubt even then that a 440 Magnum gave better and more usable performance. But the Hemi was the legend and the 440 merely an upstart in '67.

size Chryslers, where its enormous torque had been put to good use in making these heavy automobiles accelerate at respectable speeds. For the 1967 intermediates, however, the 440 Magnum had been tuned to give 375bhp instead of 350bhp, and the same vast torque enabled these lighter-bodied cars to keep pace with their Hemi-powered equivalents up to around 100mph. Few street performance enthusiasts could have wished for more, and the fact that the 440 was the largest-capacity motor yet shoehorned into an intermediate body undoubtedly gave it additional street appeal. Its pedigree was also impeccable, for the new engine was essentially an overbored version of the earlier 426 Wedge engine which had powered so many competition Dodges and Plymouths between 1963 and 1965.

The 440 came in just two models – the Plymouth Belvedere GTX and the Dodge Coronet R/T 440. The Plymouth was smaller, lighter, and faster, but the Dodge un-

doubtedly had considerable showroom appeal and probably sold rather better. Unfortunately, no figures are available to confirm this.

The GTX came as a two-door hardtop or convertible, and was introduced at the top of the Belvedere line as an image-maker for Plymouth. To that end, the division gave it a smart interior which put it in a different league to the spartan street/strip cars of the time. Similarly, Torque-Flite automatic transmission was standard, although a four-speed stick shift could be ordered instead. In stock trim, the 440-powered GTX could run quarter-miles in the mid-14s, which was fast enough for most. The Hemi option, which brought mid-13 second quarter-miles within reach, tempted fewer than one in four of those who bought a GTX during 1967.

Dodge emphasised the tractability of the 440 Magnum with a new designation for the model in which they installed it. The letters R/T in the Coronet R/T 440 name

stood for Road and Track: here, they announced, was a car which was equally at home on either. However, the car was hardly a new model, because only minor details distinguished it visually from the 1966 Coronet. Dodge knew well enough when to leave successful styling alone! Like the Plymouth GTX, the Dodge could also be had with Street Hemi power, but only 283 buyers took up that option in 1967. Most were content with the 440 Magnum's superb combination of brutal acceleration on demand with round-town driveability.

Further down the size range, however, Plymouth had pushed their Barracuda into the Muscle Car arena. The first-generation, fastback-only Barracuda had been thoroughly overshadowed by Ford's Mustang, and Chrysler were determined not to make the same mistake again. The second-generation Barracuda for 1967 had a longer wheelbase (up from 106 inches to the Mustang's 108 inches) and a wider body, which also left more room in the engine bay for large-capacity V8s. This time around, there were notchback and convertible models as well as a fastback, and the Barracuda's more rounded styling distanced it completely from the staid Valiant which provided its floorpan.

For the first time, the Barracuda could be taken seriously as a performance car. Top power option was a 383-cubic-inch V8 offering 280bhp and mid-15-second quarter-miles. It was unfortunate that the motor left no room to fit power steering, as its weight gave the top-

performance Barracuda notoriously heavy steering at low speeds. However, it no doubt played its part in boosting sales of Plymouth's ponycar, which shot up to more than 62,000 after a poor 1966 total of just 38,000.

Chevrolet

The 1967 muscle Chevrolets covered the full range of models, from the ponycar Camaro, through the intermediate Chevelle and on to the full-size Impala and Caprice. Few would argue, however, that the most important development that year was not the arrival of the Camaro – Chevy's long-awaited response to the hugely successful Ford Mustang.

LEFT: This Dodge Charger has the less powerful 318-cubic-inch engine

Chevrolet came on strong with their Camaro ponycar for '67. All the SS 396 models had identifying stripes around their noses, but only those with the Rally Sport extra-cost package came with concealed headlamps and a blacked-out grille (BELOW LEFT). Under the hood of the SS 396 (RIGHT) was Chevy's well-respected big-block V8. Even so, the hottest Camaro wasn't the SS 396 but the Z-28 developed specifically for SCCA Trans Am racing. It was also the rarest, with only 602 finding buyers in '67. The example pictured below has the Rally Sport grille-and-headlamp option.

The Z-28 Camaro had special badging (BELOW) and was the only Camaro to run the specially-developed 302 V8, which put out a lot more power than the advertised 290 horses (LEFT). The SS 396 Camaro was even chosen as the official Indianapolis Pace Car that year, which provided a lot of media exposure (RIGHT).

The Camaro arrived in September 1966, and although the base-model followed the Mustang's lead in coming with an unexciting six-cylinder motor, the top model Super Sport offered a 295bhp 350 V8 right from the beginning. Serious performance fans didn't have to wait long for more, either. A few months into the season, Chevrolet announced that an option with the Super Sport package would be the big-block 396 V8. Two states of tune were available, and the Camaro SS 396 came with either 325bhp or 375bhp. Transmissions were either a four-speed Muncie or Turbo-Hydramatic self-shifter, and several axle ratios were available to slant the SS 396's performance toward high top speeds or maximum acceleration, according to the customer's wishes. Uprated suspension came as standard (although it didn't cure the SS 396's axle hop under fierce acceleration or heavy braking) and, of course, a Positraction limited-slip differential was on the options list.

The Camaro SS 396 was the car with which Chevrolet got into the decal stripes game. Round its nose, the SS 396 had a stripe which initially distinguished it from lesser Camaros, but proved so popular that Chevrolet had to make it optional across the range before the season was over. Buyers could also order the Rally Sport option package, which gave the SS 396 a blacked-out grille and concealed headlamps.

Few people doubted that the 1967 Camaro SS 396 was a better high-performance automobile than its nearest Mustang equivalent, but Chevrolet weren't content with that. They intended to bury the Mustangs publicly, and that meant in competition. The major event for ponycars was the SCCA's new Trans Am series, and so Chevrolet set their sights on that event. However, as the GM ban on

factory competition still held, the division handed over its super-Camaro to independent racers Roger Penske and Mark Donohue.

The Trans Am rules specified that engines must be no larger than 305 cubic inches, and so Chevrolet created a 302 by fitting the short-throw crank from their 283 into the 327 block. They then added various performance accessories from the L-69 Corvette motor to produce an engine which was officially rated at 290bhp, although its actual output was very much nearer 400bhp. But the other stipulation of the Trans Am rules was that 1000 examples of the car had to be made for sale through the showrooms. As a result, the 302 became available to customers – in coupé bodies only – as Regular Production Option Z-28. Many customers probably didn't know it existed, as the Z-28 was not promoted in sales literature,

and in fact only 602 buyers were interested enough to find it and tick it in the options list on the Camaro order form.

With the right combination of carburetion and axle gearing options, a Z-28 Camaro could rip through the trap at 107mph in well under 14 seconds, although stock models were set up for high top speeds rather than maximum acceleration. In none of its guises was the 302 ever a very friendly motor, however, and Chevrolet unashamedly advertised the street-racer nature of the Camaro Z-28 by equipping the cars with broad racing stripes on hood and trunk. All the cars came with a four-speed Muncie transmission, uprated suspension, and power-assisted front disk brakes: with a 130mph top speed, the car certainly needed them!

It was no doubt to protect sales of the new Camaro that Chevrolet deleted the hottest version of its Nova SS for 1967. With the 350bhp L-79 327 motor gone, and the top option now a 275bhp 327, the performance just wasn't there and the Nova SS bowed out of the Muscle Car market after its brief appearance for 1966. The intermediate Chevelle/Malibu range was also trimmed, losing its most powerful 375bhp L-78 396 option for 1967, and topping out with a 350bhp L-34 396, 10bhp down on the '66 version. Options had street appeal: bucket seats, a center console, and a tachometer could all be had, while power-assisted front disk brakes with slotted Rally wheels and stylish red-stripe tires were a new option for 1967. A three-speed Turbo-Hydramatic also became available alongside the two-speed Powerglide for those who wanted automatic transmission.

All the full-size Chevrolets for 1967 could be had with the 325bhp 396 motor, but the most glamorous model for performance enthusiasts was the new Impala SS 427, which came with the 427-cubic-inch motor its name suggested and 385bhp. Chevrolet promoted it as a performance model, but in truth it did not have the zip now being offered by the smaller cars. In stock trim, an Impala SS 427 would run quarter-miles in the high 15s, which was quick but wasn't in the same league as the leading Muscle Cars in 1967. Chevrolet knew it, too: there was none of the smaller models' flamboyance about the SS 427, and little to distinguish the car at a distance from the more staid family sedans to which it was related.

Pontiac goes to 400 cubic inches

Riding high on the GTO's success, Pontiac would probably have changed as little as possible about their intermediate muscle model for 1967 if they had been able to have their own way. However, GM corporate policy prevented that, with the new ban on multiple carburetor set-ups which affected all 1967 models. Anxious not to lose out on performance, Pontiac were therefore forced to enlarge the venerable 389 motor so that it would give the performance of the 1966 Tri-Power option without triple carburetors.

They did it by boring the 389 out to give a full 400 cubic inches. Power outputs for 1967 remained at 1966 levels, though: the basic motor with a single Quadrajet carburetor gave the same 335bhp as the basic 389 had done, and the High Output option offered the same 360bhp as 1966's Tri-Power 389. Torque was up, however, and the 1967 GTOs could also be had with a Ram Air V8 package, which put out its 360bhp at higher revs and came with a very low axle ratio to give maximum acceleration.

Naturally, there were several axle options for the GTO,

together with a limited-slip differential option. Transmissions were a three-speed, a Muncie four-speeder for those who were serious about performance, and a Turbo-Hydramatic for those who insisted on a self-shifter. Pontiac also offered power steering, front disks with a power servo, and Rally wheels as options; and during the season, the division introduced its latest gimmick – a tachometer mounted in a pod on the hood ahead of the driver.

The lightest and cheapest of the '67 GTOs – and therefore the one most commonly equipped with all the performance goodies – was the pillared Sports Coupé, but there were also a stylish hardtop and a convertible. Styling reflected the division's recognition that the car already had plenty of sales appeal, and the only exterior changes for '67 were to front and rear details, while there were also minor interior revisions. Perhaps they weren't enough, though, because GTO sales were down for '67 on their '66 peak. The competition was catching up.

Of course, some GTO sales might well have been lost to

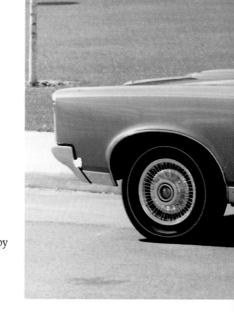

The Camaro Z-28 wasn't for everybody, and the kid in the street was in any case pretty happy to get the latest Pontiac GTO (RIGHT AND BELOW), now with a 400-cubic-inch motor and improved torque.

The 1967 Pontiac Firebird (BELOW)
was very closely related to the
Chevrolet Camaro, and could be
bought with the 400-cubic-inch V8.
The '67 Firebird convertible
(OVERLEAF) has a middle-of-the-
range 326-cubic-inch V8.

Pontiac's own Firebird, which appeared in February 1967 and achieved no fewer than 82,000 sales before the season was out. Based on the Chevrolet Camaro platform, and sharing many details with that car, the Firebird was Pontiac's first entry into the ponycar market. Following the standard ponycar profile, it came in base-model form with an uninspiring straight-six motor, but right from the beginning the top performance option was Pontiac's new 400-cubic-inch V8.

As the Firebird was considerably lighter than the GTO, it didn't need the same power to achieve high performance, and so the 400 came with just 325bhp in basic form. A second version of the engine, offered like the GTO high-performance package with Ram Air, gave the same 325bhp but at higher revs, and was allied to a lowered axle ratio to give the car quarter-mile times in the mid-14s at around 100mph. It wasn't as fast as a GTO on the strip, but then Pontiac knew that its main appeal was to the street crowd, and here the ponycar scored with zero to 60 times which would leave even a good GTO struggling. However, it took a good driver to get the best out of a hot '67 Firebird, because the high-performance versions of the car suffered from bad axle tramp under fierce acceleration; in most street playoffs, a GTO was likely to win out.

The Firebird could be bought with all the obligatory '67 goodies. Options included front disks, mag rally wheels,

This 1967 Oldsmobile 4-4-2 convertible wears the red stripe tires and wire-spoke wheel covers which were fashionable in its day (LEFT).

Some performance enthusiasts preferred to create their own muscle machinery out of more ordinary cars. This Mercury Cougar (RIGHT) has been considerably modified in the spirit of the Muscle Car era.

and Pontiac's new tacho-on-the-hood. Always more expensive than its close cousin the Camaro, the Firebird never made quite the same impact on the popular imagination – but it was certainly a machine to be reckoned with on the street in '67.

Buick and Oldsmobile

The other two GM divisions which fielded Muscle Cars for 1967 didn't quite have the success of Pontiac and Chevrolet. Buick dropped a new motor into their Skylark GS to give the car extra go, and Oldsmobile managed to achieve better sales of their 4-4-2 than in 1966. Both cars were good, but neither was in the front row of the Muscle Car pack.

Maximum performance of the Oldsmobile was actually down on '66 levels because the L-69 triple-deuce package had fallen victim to the GM ban on multiple carburetor set-ups. Persistent customers could still obtain the drag-racing W-30 package, but for street use the top of the range was the 350bhp 400 motor. As the 4-4-2 was a relatively heavy car, performance was not startling, and the car could only just break the 16-second quarter-mile barrier in stock trim.

There was more excitement to be had over at Buick, who had thoroughly revamped their hot Skylark for '67. For a start, it wasn't a Skylark any more, but rather a GS-400, with the numbers reflecting the capacity of its new semi-wedge-head V8 motor. The old nail-head 401 had gone, to be replaced by a higher-revving engine which pumped out the same 340bhp but a fraction less torque. Performance was now competitive with the rest of the field. Three-speed stick shift and Super Turbine automatic transmissions could be had, and the top-

option Muncie four-speed and optional Positive Traction limited-slip differential helped to make a GS-400 one of the fastest of the '67 muscle models on the street, with a zero to 60mph time of just six seconds. Later in the season Buick capitalized on their new model's success by offering a cheaper 260bhp GS-340 alongside the GS-400. But it wasn't fast enough for those tempted by the GS badge, and it didn't sell.

Ford, Mercury, and Shelby

Ford still didn't really count on the street in 1967. The Fairlane 427, introduced a year earlier, was still available but probably didn't attract more than 200 buyers. Not that there was anything wrong with the car – far from it, in fact, as the side-oiler 427 still gave 410bhp in regular tune and 425bhp with dual-quad Holleys – but the problem was that it didn't really have an image. Ford tried hard in competition, but couldn't beat the MOPARs on the strips, and couldn't maintain the momentum of their Daytona 500 win with a much-modified Fairlane. For street use, the '67 Fairlane 427 came with a steel hood, although drag-racers could still order the lighter fiberglass hood which had been standard on '66 models.

Ford also put Mercury badges on the Fairlane's bodyshell for 1967, and offered the car in slightly more luxurious and more expensive form as the Comet Cyclone GT. A few – probably 50 – were equipped with the side-oiler 427 and 425bhp, but these were professional competition machines. For the street, the Mercury came with the same 390 motor as the Fairlane GT, which gave quick rather than Muscle Car performance. Like the Fairlanes themselves, the Mercurys did little for Ford's high-performance image.

1967 was the last year when the Shelby Mustangs were actually built by Shelby-American in Los Angeles. Although the '67 GT-350 had all the right trimmings – mag wheels (LEFT) and racing decals (BELOW), it had taken another step away from Carroll Shelby's original concept as seen on the '65 models. This model looks good in its red and white finish (ABOVE RIGHT), but the addition of a more comfortable and luxurious interior (BELOW RIGHT) showed the way Ford wanted to go with future high-performance Mustangs.

There was nothing wrong with Carroll Shelby's image for '67, though, and the Shelby-developed Mustangs actually offered even more performance this season. They shared the regular Mustang's new longer and wider body, but all had a unique frontal treatment with two driving lamps ahead of the grille; and, as before, all were 2+2 fastback models.

The GT-350 model continued, still with the 306bhp 289 under its hood, but the big news was that there was now also a GT-500 model, equipped with Ford's new Police Interceptor 428 motor with two four-barrel Holleys and a 355bhp output. Although this was a heavier and more expensive car than the GT-350, it was also a lot quicker, and the attractions of quarter-miles in the mid-14s at more than 100mph were enough for the GT-500 to outsell the GT-350 by two to one during 1967.

Some customers just had to have more, however, and a couple of Ford dealerships offered converted GT-500s with the Ford 427 in place of the 428. Power and performance increases were much as might be expected with an extra 70bhp and 60lbf ft of torque, but not many of these so-called "Shelby Super Snakes" were made – possibly no more than 20, and certainly not more than 50.

Many enthusiasts insist that 1967 was the last year for the real Shelby Mustangs, because production was transferred from Shelby's Los Angeles premises to a Ford sub-contractor in Michigan at the end of the year, and because for 1968 the Shelby Mustangs were markedly more Ford

and less Shelby. But the rot had actually set in even earlier. The 1967 cars were a whole lot more civilized than the original Shelbys, with much higher trim levels as standard, and they could be ordered with luxury goodies like air conditioning and power steering, which had no place in the original Shelby street-racer concept. Even so, the '67 Shelby Mustangs were fast enough on the street to give their owners the fun they expected.

Muscle Car Choice – 1967

Ponycars
Chevrolet Camaro SS 396
Chevrolet Camaro Z-28
Plymouth Barracuda
(with 383 option)
Pontiac Firebird (with
400 or 326 Ho option)
Shelby Mustang GT-350
Shelby Mustang GT-500

Intermediates
Buick GS-400
Chevrolet Malibu SS 396
Dodge Charger
(with Hemi option)
Dodge Coronet R/T 440
Ford Fairlane 427
Mercury Comet Cyclone
GT (with 427 option)
Oldsmobile 4-4-2
Plymouth Belvedere GTX
(with 440 or Hemi option)
Plymouth Satellite
(with Hemi option)
Pontiac GTO

Full-size
Chevrolet Impala SS 427

1968
More Regulations

Muscle Car fans felt the cold wind of change blowing as the 1968 season opened, for the '68 models were the first ones to be subject to the Federal regulations governing automotive safety and exhaust emissions. The long-term effects of those regulations were undoubtedly beneficial, but in the beginning they were very much disliked, and few car buyers disliked them as much as those in the market for a Muscle Car. The reasons were straightforward enough: most of the changes mandated for '68 added both weight and cost, both of which went against everything the Muscle Cars stood for.

There were no loopholes in these new rules to help the Muscle Car makers, and the '68 models followed the new safety regulations with their side marker lights, dual brake circuits, front shoulder belts, laminated windshields, and anti-burst door locks. As yet, the exhaust emissions control regulations were not too severe – though they would be tightened progressively as the

years went on – and so the Muscle Cars did not suffer from the wholesale power and performance losses which would gradually diminish their appeal.

Their appeal was nevertheless on the wane, and one major reason was that insurance companies had started to raise the premiums on high-performance cars. Their reasoning was that young drivers in high-performance cars had more than their share of accidents which were followed by insurance claims, and so premiums had to go up to cover the increased risk that the insurers would have to meet a claim. Muscle Car buyers were predominantly young, and most of them did not have a lot of spare cash. As a result, increasing numbers found themselves unable to afford the insurance premiums on a Muscle Car, and they therefore had to settle for something tamer and less costly to insure.

There was more, though. Muscle Cars had been getting gradually more expensive over the years, as customers

Plymouth's Road Runner was the first of a new breed of budget-Muscle Cars, but not many looked as mean as this one (ABOVE RIGHT), which had the optional 426 Hemi motor, which was fitted to just 1019 examples that year. For '68, the 426 Hemi was still pumping out 425bhp at 5000rpm and 490lbf ft of torque at 4000rpm (LEFT).

RIGHT: This 318-cubic-inch Dodge Charger could not make that year's Scat Pack, but was still a fine-looking car.

Plymouth – bargain muscle

Plymouth really got it right in '68, aiming three attractive models at the street crowd. Smallest was the Barracuda, still on a 108-inch wheelbase and a strong contender in the ponycar market. Familiar as a model from '67, but restyled and much more successful in the marketplace this year, was the GTX. And then there was the Road Runner.

The Road Runner took its name from the Warner Brothers cartoon character whose cunning and speed always allowed him to escape from his enemy, the coyote, and it came complete with a horn which mimicked the character's distinctive "beep-beep." These were marketing gimmicks, however. The essence of the car was the lightest version of the restyled '68 Belvedere body (the pillared coupé), stripped to essentials to save weight and cost, and equipped with a high-torque 335bhp version of Plymouth's 383-cubic-inch V8. In the spring of 1968, with the Road Runner well established as a model, an alternative pillarless coupé version was also introduced.

The Road Runner's 383 was very different from the 383 found in other Plymouths, mainly because it had been modified with a number of parts from the big 440 Super Commando V8. In outright performance terms, it didn't give the Road Runner the edge on more expensive muscle machinery, but with 0 to 60 times of under 7.5 seconds and quarter-miles of under 15.5 seconds at nearly 100mph, it was fast enough to offer the fun which young street fans wanted. Sales were overwhelmingly successful. Plymouth had predicted first-year sales of 2500, but by the end of the '68 season, the division had shipped over 44,000 Road Runners to grateful customers!

had demanded bigger and more powerful engines, and more and more street-appeal or convenience features. It was Plymouth who first tackled the problem, by introducing the Road Runner, the pioneer "budget" Muscle Car. Built down to a price, this model took the Muscle Car scene by storm during 1968, vastly exceeded its makers' sales estimates, and set a new trend which other manufacturers were not slow to follow. In its own way, the Plymouth Road Runner was as important in the evolution of the Muscle Car as Chevrolet's 409 of 1961 or Pontiac's GTO of 1964.

Yet by the end of the 1968 season, a disturbing trend was emerging. It was becoming increasingly clear that performance alone was not the major factor in determining sales of a Muscle Car. Several of 1968's models were slower than their 1967 predecessors, but still out-sold them. Attractive styling, the image of a name, and clever marketing seemed to have moved in on the performance market this year.

Of course, the Road Runner's low sticker price was only there to tempt buyers into the showrooms. Plymouth knew that buyers hooked on the basic concept of their bargain Muscle Car would probably order a fistful of extras, and so there was a long option list, and not many Road Runners were sold in "pure" form. Just over 1000 richer buyers opted to have their Road Runners equipped with the 426 Street Hemi instead of the 383 motor, and these cars were much more convincing at the strips. However, they weren't really what the Road Runner was all about.

Like the Road Runner, the '68 GTX had the new and softer styling introduced that year for the Belvedere line. That styling was probably the reason why sales were so much better than those for the previous season, because powertrain choices remained the same, with the 375bhp 440 Super Commando V8 as standard and the 425bhp Hemi for serious strip performance. The majority of the 19,000 GTX models for '68 were hardtop coupés, but just over 1000 buyers were tempted by the convertible body. Only 450 buyers ordered their GTXs with Hemi power, which reflected the specialized-use nature of that option.

Top of the power options for the Barracuda ponycar was once again the 383 V8, which boasted a power increase to 300bhp from last year's 280bhp, but was still nothing like as powerful as the 383 developed for the Road Runner. Even though a 383-powered Barracuda was several hundred pounds lighter than even a stripped-out Road Runner, it therefore didn't deliver astounding performance. Quarter-miles in the high 15s and zero to 60 in just under 7.5 seconds were very much under par in a season when the leading street/strip machines were running quarter-miles in the low 14s and streaking to 60mph in just over six seconds.

To give the Barracuda an image boost, Plymouth therefore had a few Hemi-powered Barracudas built for strip use by the professionals. Assembly of these Super Stock Hemi Barracudas was sub-contracted to Hurst Performance, and the cars were stripped out as far as possible so that they still remained street-legal. Whether they would actually have been driveable on the street is another question, however, as they were very highly tuned. Strip performance was predictably shattering, with 10-second quarters and terminal speeds of 130mph. But the gap between this kind of performance and that of the everyday Barracuda was enormous.

Dodge – the Scat Pack

Dodge adopted a new marketing strategy for '68, grouping its Muscle Cars together under the promotional banner of the Scat Pack and using a picture of a bee as an identifying logo. High-performance Coronets, Chargers, and Darts all came as standard with "bumble-bee" racing stripe decals around their tails to distinguish them from their lesser brethren, although buyers who preferred a low-key approach could have the stripes deleted.

Chrysler's Plymouth and Dodge divisions tended to do things as a couple, and so it wasn't at all surprising to find Dodge shadowing the Plymouth Road Runner with their own budget street racer. But they didn't get the balance quite right: their Coronet Super Bee was more expensive than the Road Runner, and had a plusher interior and a softer ride. While these qualities were undoubtedly highly desirable in themselves, they didn't win over quite as many of the drive-in crowd, who saw the more spartan, rough-riding Road Runner as closer to a dragstrip special.

The Coronet Super Bee came with the same 335bhp 383 motor as the Road Runner, and it was capable of quarter-miles at a fraction over 14 seconds with a trap speed of nearly 100mph. For its price, this was heady stuff; and although the Super Bee could also be bought with Hemi power and even more performance, that option was expensive enough to rob the car of its budget-muscle appeal. But the Super Bee wasn't everyone's idea of a fast Coronet in '68, in any case. Buyers who wanted a few more creature comforts – air conditioning, power windows, and automatic transmission – could still order a very quick machine in the shape of the Coronet R/T.

This came as a hardtop or a convertible, with the new styling which graced all the '68 Coronet range and a hood

For 1968, Plymouth's GTX had new styling around the same power packages as had been offered for '67. This example, pictured above, has the rare 426 Hemi option, generally ordered only for dragstrip use. Under its hood, the motor looked much the same as it did in other MOPAR muscle machines of the time (RIGHT).

Everything red-and-white, plus the Scat Pack identifiers of bumble-bee stripes, made this '68 Dodge Charger (OVERLEAF) stand out from the crowd; the 440 Magnum V8 in this example promised 375bhp.

bulge unique to the R/T and Super Bee. However, power-trains were unchanged from last season. For most buyers, that meant the 440 Magnum engine with 375bhp, which gave quarter-miles in the mid-14s at around 97mph. At extra cost, of course, the evergreen Hemi could be dropped into the engine bay to produce a strip scorcher.

The Charger, too, had new sheet metal for 1968, and now came with very attractive new "coke-bottle" styling on the same 117-inch wheelbase. It had a semi-fastback roof with flying-buttress sail panels and a recessed back-light, and its rear end kicked up into the merest hint of a tail spoiler. A black grille with hidden headlamps came as standard. Most important for performance enthusiasts, though, it could now be bought with the R/T package pioneered on the '67 Coronet.

A Charger R/T came with the 375bhp 440 Magnum engine, a Torque-Flite automatic transmission with raised "competition" shift speeds (a four-speed manual was optional), heavy-duty brakes with a front disk and power assistance option, and a handling package. In stock trim, it was good for quarter-miles in the mid-14s at 98mph. As usual, those who wanted more acceleration

could order their chargers with Hemi power, which brought quarter-miles down below 14 seconds and put terminal speeds up by around 6mph. Hemi Chargers com-peted in NASCAR events, but didn't do as well as they might because the ruling authority demanded that the Hemi had to be fitted with carburetor restriction plates.

The third model in the Scat Pack was the Dart, now in GT Sport (or GTS) guise and offering much greater per-formance than before. Earlier Darts had been quick, but hardly qualified as Muscle Cars; for '68, however, a pair of muscular V8s changed all that.

The Dart sat on a 111-inch wheelbase, and was con-siderably lighter than the Chargers and Coronets with their 117-inch wheelbases. It therefore needed less power and torque to make it move quickly, and in fact the engine in the regular GTS was a 340 which was officially rated at just 275bhp. That rating was certainly an under-estimate, however, and there isn't much doubt that the engine's true output was nearer 330bhp. One way or an-other, it had enough urge to power a GTS Dart to quarter-miles in the mid-14s at nearly 100mph, which was well up with the leading streetable machines for '68.

No one could have failed to recognize the performance pretensions of this 1968 Dodge Charger R/T at a glance – and there was just as much go as there was show (RIGHT). With the 440 Magnum, a Charger could run quarter-miles in the high 14s at 98mph. For ultimate performance, though, it still had to be the Hemi. Pictured below is one of 475 Charger R/Ts equipped with that engine. Its 425bhp brought quarter-mile times down to 13.5 seconds at over 100mph (BELOW RIGHT).

AMC were on target with their new AMX for 1968, which not only looked good (BELOW RIGHT) but also had promising performance from its 390-cubic-inch V8 (LEFT). On the right is one of the rare Dodge Darts fitted with the 440 Magnum V8 and intended for strip use. The big motor was transplanted straight from larger Dodges, such as the Charger R/T where one is seen in the picture below.

Even faster was a GTS equipped with the 335bhp 383 motor, although performance differences were not that great. Still, the Dart GTS 383 remained a streetable machine, which was more than could be said for the drag-strip specials which Dodge prepared for a limited number of professional drivers. These came in two forms. Forty-eight cars were built with the 375bhp 440 Magnum V8, and a smaller number of Hemi Darts were built with 425bhp motors. Between them, they helped to keep the Dart in the public eye at NHRA events.

AMC – the newcomer

Nineteen sixty-eight was undoubtedly Chrysler's year once again as far as muscle fans were concerned, but a great deal of attention was also paid to a deserving new-comer from American Motors. The American Motors corporation, or AMC, had been formed as long ago as 1954 from the merger of Nash and Hudson, but it had seen lean times in the early 1960s when it had clung to compacts as the American public turned away from them. For that reason, it had never entered the Muscle Car arena – until now.

AMC's revival had begun in the mid-1960s and had taken a sharp upturn at the beginning of the '68 season as the Javelin fastback ponycar replaced the Marlin which had started the revival. But the company's masterstroke was not revealed until mid-season, when the AMX was announced. To make sure customers sat up and took notice, AMC introduced the car with an announcement that speed star Craig Breedlove had already used one to set no fewer than 106 speed records.

There was nothing else quite like the AMX available from domestic manufacturers. In essence, it was a Javelin with 12 inches sliced from the middle to give a sporty two-seater on a 97-inch wheelbase. The only other two-seater then being built in the U.S. was the Chevrolet Cor-

vette, which was in a different category altogether, and the AMX certainly scored by being different. But it also scored because it offered high performance in a compact and stylish package.

There were three choices of engine for the '68 AMX, all V8s, but the most popular was the largest of them, with 390 cubic inches, 315bhp, and impressive amounts of torque. As often as not, this was specified as part of the optional "Go" package, which brought front disk brakes with power assistance, heavy-duty suspension, a Twin-Grip differential, and a few other goodies, which included racing stripes for street appeal. Standard transmission was a rather woolly four-speed manual, but a three-speed Shift Command automatic with a floor shifter was optional, and buyers could also order more precise steering with or without power assistance. There were several optional axle ratios, too, in the best Muscle Car tradition.

Respectably quick in the 0 to 60mph dash, the AMX was less impressive on the strips, where stock versions ran quarter-miles in the high 14s at 95mph. But that didn't seem to deter the buyers, even though sales for '68 fell short of AMC's hopes for the car.

GM – Buick and Oldsmobile

The intermediate ranges into which the majority of GM's Muscle Cars fell were all reduced in size for 1968, as 1967's 115-inch wheelbases shrank to 112 inches and new sheet metal was prescribed for all divisions. Inevitably, this affected every one of the General's intermediate Muscle Cars, and the 1968 Chevrolet Chevelle, Pontiac GTO, Buick GS, and Oldsmobile 4-4-2 were all smaller than their 1967 incarnations.

Despite this reduction in size, a '68 Buick GS-400 was a few pounds heavier than a '67. As the division had not managed to come up with a new engine at the top of the range, performance suffered accordingly. Nevertheless, sales held up to very much the same levels as for '67, and so it must have been the car's attractive new styling which kept the public interested. Lower down the scale, the GS-350, which had replaced last year's GS-340, did very well indeed, although it couldn't even equal the GS-400's quarter-mile times, which now barely scraped below the 16-second barrier. Either Buick buyers didn't really want performance for '68, or the division was no longer prepared to give it to them. . . .

By contrast, Oldsmobile managed to make their 4-4-2 go very much faster than in '67. Along with the rest of the F-85 and Cutlass line, the car had curvaceous new styling with a semi-fastback roof and what became known as a "bullet" profile. For '68, however, the 4-4-2 became a separate series of its own for the first time. Lightest and cheapest was the pillared coupé, next up came a pillarless Holiday Coupé, and top of the price and the weight lists was a convertible.

The new styling certainly played its part, pushing '68 sales up over 33,000 from the 25,000 achieved in 1967, but equally important must have been the 4-4-2's new engine. Still with the 400 cubic inches of last year's displacement, it had nevertheless been extensively reworked with a narrower bore and longer stroke, new cylinder heads with modified ports, and a more radical camshaft. Like the '67 motor, it gave 350bhp when mated to a manual transmission (three-speed or Muncie four-speed), but this time around it was detuned to just 325bhp when the optional Turbo Hydramatic transmission was specified.

There were options, of course. Force-Air induction (which consisted of a pair of vulnerable-looking air scoops mounted below the bumper) boosted power to 360bhp, but the top option was the W-30 package. No longer a dragstrip special, the W-30 was a street scorcher with the 360bhp Force-Air 400 and a few other modifications, not the least of which as far as the street crowd were concerned was a pair of identifying patches in contrasting paint on the hood. However, the W-30 was no drive-in special, either: it would reach 60mph in six seconds dead and power on to 13-second quarter-miles at 105mph. The good handling associated with all 4-4-2s helped to make this Oldsmobile one of 1968's best Muscle Cars.

Even so, Oldsmobile topped it toward the end of the season. George Hurst, of the Hurst Performance Shifter company, modified his own 4-4-2 by fitting it with the big 455-cubic-inch V8 from an Oldsmobile Toronado. So impressed were the factory engineers that Oldsmobile decided to run off a limited number of 455-powered Hurst/Olds 4-4-2s for sale through selected dealerships. The version of the 455 which ended up in these cars was in fact not quite the same as that in the big Toronado, and no other Oldsmobile of the time had it in the same 390bhp, 500lbf ft state of tune. Nor could Oldsmobile themselves find room to assemble the cars, sub-contracting production instead to an engineering firm in Lansing, Michigan. Just 515 Hurst/Olds were built before the end of the season, but they were not the last 4-4-2s to run the big 455 V8: the model had proved popular enough for Oldsmobile to retain it for the 1969 model line-up.

GM – Chevrolet

The 1968 Chevrolet Muscle Cars centered on the 396-cubic-inch motor, which was by now in its fourth season as a performance engine. Chevrolet offered it in their 119-inch-wheelbase full-size ranges, in the 112-inch-wheel-

Stripes again, this time around on the front of a 1968 Oldsmobile 4-4-2 (BELOW). Engine revisions probably helped boost sales just as much as the improved styling for '68: although the power output remained the same as in '67, maximum torque came in at lower engine speeds on the later cars. The V8 engine still displaced 400 cubic inches, although bore and stroke had both been altered (RIGHT).

Chevrolet's 396 V8 could be had in the division's compacts, ponycars, intermediates, *and* full-size models. The compact Nova SS 396 (ABOVE) was new to the range, and capitalized on its small size and light weight, while the Chevelle SS 396 (LEFT) was by now an established intermediate contender. The 396 wasn't the top option for the large and heavy Impalas, though (ABOVE LEFT), which needed the more muscular 427 to give them real performance. Few buyers bothered, and the Impala SS 427 didn't last beyond the middle of 1969.

base Chevelle, in the 111-inch-wheelbase Nova, and in the 108.1-inch Camaro. But it wasn't the only performance motor from GM's best-selling division. Full-size models could still be ordered with the 427, and there was also the 302, which remained exclusive to the Z-28 Camaro.

In the full-size ranges, the 427 was becoming increasingly scarce. Chevrolet didn't bother to increase its power from 1967's 385bhp, and fewer and fewer buyers thought it worthwhile buying a large car with a large engine which could be shut down by most other cars with any real pretensions to performance. The 396 simply didn't rate as a performance engine in the large and heavy Biscaynes, Bel Airs, Impalas, and Caprices, not least because in these cars it came in its lowest state of tune with just 325bhp.

The Chevelle intermediates, newly restyled for 1968, of course once again included an SS 396 model, and in fact the SS 396 became a separate series for the first time this year. All three states of 396 tune were available in the Chevelle SS – 325bhp, 350bhp L-34, and 375bhp L-78, the latter capable of propelling a hardtop to 14-second quarter-miles at 100mph with the right axle ratio.

The smaller Nova, never a Muscle Car contender in previous years, joined the high-performance Chevrolets at mid-season when the 350bhp and 375bhp versions of the 396 V8 became optional in the Nova SS coupé. With the most powerful engine option, quarter-miles in the mid-14s at over 100mph were possible, but their late in-

Chevrolet continued to promote the Camaro as a muscle machine for 1968, making few changes to the appearance as compared to the original '67 cars. The SS trim continued to make Camaros look hot, although the SS 350 pictured below didn't qualify among the fastest models with its 295bhp, 350-cubic-inch V8. Real performance came from the SS 396, pictured right, and from the Z-28 (LEFT) with its 302 V8 originally developed for the SCCA's Trans Am series.

troduction prevented more than 6571 Nova SS coupés from finding buyers before the end of the season. Of these, just 667 had the 375bhp option.

Unlike the intermediates, the ponycar Camaro was barely altered for 1968. Chevrolet did cure its axle hop by fitting multiple-leaf rear springs and staggered dampers, but otherwise the main news was that the Camaro SS could be ordered in three states of tune instead of last year's two. The new one was the intermediate 350bhp tune. The Camaro SS 396 was respectably quick, but even with the 375bhp engine it took nearly 15 seconds to run the quarter-mile. Not so the Z-28 model, however, still offered with its special 302 motor and still not mentioned in Camaro sales literature. With the right axle ratio and dealer-installed stock power modifications, the Z-28 could storm through the traps in the high 13s at 107mph. On the street, the Z-28 still looked the part, with its broad stripes on hood and trunk lid, and sub-seven-second 0 to 60mph times ensured that it was not to be trifled with.

GM – Pontiac

Pontiac entered 1968 with the same Muscle Car line-up as in the previous season – the Firebird ponycar and the GTO intermediate. The GTO, however, was very different from the '67 model, with exciting new styling on its newly shortened wheelbase.

An instant recognition feature of the '68 GTO was its energy-absorbing front bumper, made of body-colored Endura and styled into the nose of the car as a grille surround with three hefty "overriders" – one ahead of each fender and one in the center of the grille. In outline, both hardtop coupé and convertible styles were similar to the other GM intermediate Muscle Cars for '68, but the GTO scored with its squarer wheel arches and an altogether more muscular appearance. Standard bucket seats and a first-class instrument display rounded off another excellent edition of the famous intermediate which had started the whole genre.

Nothing is perfect, of course, and the '68 GTO had put on weight. To counter the effects of that, Pontiac had beefed-up the base 400-cubic-inch V8 by 15bhp to give 350bhp, although the performance options of the four-barrel 400 HO and Ram Air versions still gave the same 360bhp as before. After March 1969, new cylinder heads, lightweight valves, and a number of other modifications turned the Ram Air motor into a Ram Air II, although official power ratings remained unchanged.

A Ram Air GTO was good for quarter-miles in the mid-14s at around 98mph and needed around 6.5 seconds to reach 60mph from rest. It was fast, but there were faster machines on the street that year. Yet, once again, it seemed to be image and appearance as much as real performance which were selling cars in 1968, and GTO sales were up by around 6000 over 1967, to 87,684.

As the Firebird had enjoyed only half a season in 1967, it was hardly surprising to find it barely altered for 1968. Just as on the Camaro, its unhappy rear suspension had been sorted by the addition of multiple-leaf springs and staggered dampers. As far as power was concerned, the 400 had been persuaded to yield an extra 5bhp in base form, taking it up to 330bhp, and last season's two engine options were now up to three. The 400 HO option weighed-in with 335bhp, and the top option for acceleration was the Ram-Air 400, promising the same 335bhp but at higher revolutions.

Pontiac's 1968 GTO had gorgeous new fastback styling, although the revised sheet metal did add weight. The front end pictures on this page show quite clearly the "Endura" nosepiece with its three protective projections, while the rear view (BELOW RIGHT) emphasizes the car's squat and powerful appearance.

The Firebird (ABOVE RIGHT) remained available in both open and closed forms, now with a slightly more powerful 400-cubic-inch V8 as the top performance option.

. . . and Ford

Ford dominated the NASCAR championships this year with the newly-restyled Ford Torino and Mercury Cyclone fastbacks, but they were also-rans once again in 1968 as far as street performance fans were concerned. The Fairlane 427 did remain available for the first half of the season, until December 1967, but it made no more impact on the street than it had done in earlier times. As for Mercury division, lower-powered Comet Cyclones with no more than 390bhp did it no favors on the street or the strip. So once again, the real performance Fords came with Shelby badges.

As had been the case during '67, both GT-350 and GT-500 versions of the Shelby Mustang were offered, although this season a convertible bodyshell was also available and the cars were officially known as Shelby Cobras. Distinctive features were rectangular driving lamps ahead of the grille and a more accentuated grille opening. The 306bhp 289-cubic-inch motor in the GT-350 gave way to a 250bhp 302, but power in the GT-500 went up slightly, from 355bhp to 360bhp. Ford Division had a much greater hand in the creation of these Shelbys than in the 1965-1967 cars, though, and the '68s were assembled by a company in Ionia, Michigan rather than by Shelby-American.

The Cougar was Mercury's entry into the ponycar stakes, but it never sold as well as its Mustang cousin from Ford. Top performer in 1968 was the Cougar GTE (BELOW LEFT), which sported a 390bhp edition of the Ford 427 motor (LEFT).

With the top-option 360bhp 428 motor (RIGHT), a Shelby Cobra GT-500 was a desirable performance model in 1968 (BELOW AND OVERLEAF), but Carroll Shelby's involvement with the cars which bore his name was growing smaller.

The King of the Road or GT-500KR version of the Shelby Mustang went on to become one of the most prized classic cars of the 1960s. Just 933 fastbacks like the example pictured (LEFT AND OVERLEAF) were built, together with 318 convertibles. The Ram-Air hood and special side stripe (ABOVE) made them instantly recognizable. Performance came from the 428 Cobra-Jet motor, conservatively rated by Ford at 335bhp.

In April, however, a brand-new Shelby Mustang replaced the GT-500. This one was equipped with the Ram Air 428 Cobra Jet motor which had already been seen in competition Mustangs in the NHRA's Super Stock classes. Official figures claimed just 335bhp, but few people doubted that this latest big-block put out something very much closer to 400bhp. Not for nothing was the newcomer known as the GT-500KR (those additional letters stood for "King of the Road"), and quarter-mile times of a fraction over 14 seconds with a trap speed of well over 100mph demonstrated that Ford did have the material to build a decent Muscle Car, even though they still wanted to hide it behind Shelby badges.

The good-looking new fastback on the 116-inch intermediates wasn't one of those cars the street fans loved, although in later years it would have more appeal. Ford offered it on the Torino GT and Fairlane models, and it could also be had with cosmetic changes as a Mercury Cyclone GT. In fact, the Cyclone's different grille helped high-speed aerodynamics, with the result that the Mercury racers were faster in NASCAR events. However, it was Ford who won the championship, and driver David Pearson who took individual honors.

The big fastbacks were available initially with the 390bhp 427 V8, and the Torino and Cyclone (though not the Fairlane 500) later took on the 428 Cobra Jet motor with its advertised 335bhp. This year, none of them made a really big splash on the street, but greater things were in store for Ford's new intermediate coupés.

Muscle Car Choice – 1968

Subcompacts
AMC AMX 390

Compacts
Chevrolet Nova SS 396
Dodge Dart GTS

Ponycars
Chevrolet Camaro SS 396
Chevrolet Camaro Z-28
Plymouth Barracuda
(with 383 option)
Pontiac Firebird
(with 400 option)
Shelby Mustang GT-500
Shelby Mustang
GT-500KR

Intermediates
Buick GS-400
Chevrolet Chevelle SS 396
Dodge Coronet R/T
Dodge Coronet Super Bee
Ford Torino GT
(with 427 or 428 option)
Mercury Cyclone GT
(with 427 or 428 option)
Oldsmobile 4-4-2
Plymouth GTX
Plymouth Road Runner
Pontiac GTO

Full-size
Chevrolet Impala SS 427

1969

Budget Muscle and Aerodynamics

The subtle Muscle Car had gone by 1969. The market no longer wanted the Q-ships of the early 1960s, stripped-out stock sedans with big-block motors which would blow the doors off unsuspecting sportscars when the traffic lights turned green. Instead, it wanted bold graphics, bright colors, hood scoops, and mag-style wheels. More than one motor manufacturer made a fast buck or two in 1969 from models which had all the right appearance addenda but didn't have top-option muscle motors under their hoods.

Flavor of the year were the new budget muscle models, created in the wake of Plymouth's Road Runner. Dodge followed through with the Super Bee, Pontiac had their GTO Judge, Ford their Cobra 428, and Chevrolet tried hard with their Nova SS. But the most sensational trend was toward aerodynamic addenda, encouraged by the need to minimize air drag at the very high speeds attained by NASCAR racers. Dodge tried but failed to match the sleek Fords and Mercurys with their Charger 500, and then came back later in the season with the astonishing Charger Daytona which sported aerodynamic aids the street crowd loved. Even so, it was the Fords which triumphed at NASCAR; Dodge came a good second, although for 1970 things would be different.

The aerodynamic addenda on this Dodge Daytona were originally developed to improve the car's chances on the high-speed ovals in NASCAR racing (MAIN PICTURE). Nevertheless, it was the fastback Ford intermediates which took the honors in 1969 with hot versions of cars like the Torino GT in the foreground of the picture above. Alongside is a Fairlane Cobra, an attractive fastback aimed at the budget-muscle market.

Ford and Mercury come good

Nineteen sixty-nine was the year in which a lot of things worked out right for Ford and for its Mercury division. The president since early 1968 had been "Bunkie" Knudsen, the former Pontiac chief who had been recruited to improve Ford's performance image, and that image certainly did start to look up during 1969. At long last, Ford had the cars which mattered on the street, as well as those which mattered on the tracks. And they really did matter on the tracks – for the second year running, Ford won the NASCAR Manufacturers' Championship and Ford driver David Pearson won the drivers' title.

Dearborn had the high-performance scene well covered for '69. At the cheap end of the market, they countered Plymouth's Road Runner with the new Cobra 428; new muscle Mustangs eclipsed the Shelby models, which were now in their last season; and on the NASCAR ovals, the Torino Talladega proved very hard to beat. Mercurys were also attractive propositions, with the Cyclone coming as a Talladega equivalent and the Cougar Eliminator an interesting but not always convincing upscale ponycar. Common to both divisions was the enormously powerful new Boss 429 "semi-hemi" motor, developed for the NASCAR tracks and seen in Mustangs, Talladegas, and Mercury Cyclones.

Central to Ford's performance range for 1969 was the Torino fastback, newly rechristened the SportsRoof but otherwise very similar to its 1968 incarnation. This stylish intermediate, which sat on a 116-inch wheelbase, spawned both the budget street-or-strip Cobra 428, with which Ford took on the Plymouth Road Runner, and the NASCAR-special Torino Talladega. The more affordable of the two was of course the Cobra 428, a no-frills Muscle Car with the 335bhp Cobra Jet 428 motor, four-speed transmission, and heavy-duty suspension as standard. Even in standard form, it could run quarter-miles in the mid-14s at 100mph, whch made it a more than worthy competitor for the hot GM intermediates. There was even more performance available from the optional Ram Air 428 engine, known as the CJ-R and advertised with the same 335bhp as the regular 428 – the hood scoop which came as part of this package gave a welcome dose of street appeal as well as extra performance.

The Torino Talladega, by contrast, was only offered through the showrooms so that it could be raced in NASCAR events. Named after the new Alabama track which opened in 1969, it was Ford's answer to the Dodge Charger 500. In the interests of greater high-speed performance, it had been lowered by an inch on its suspension and sported a lengthened and tapered nose with a flush grille and special bumper. None of these modifications made any difference to acceleration on the street but, together with the matt black hood panel, they certainly looked the business. Once again, appearance counted for a lot, and these cars in stock form for the street were not as fast as they looked: quarter-miles in the low 14s at 101mph were impressive, but not exceptional for this time.

Ford had some hugely attractive contenders in the muscle market for 1969. The Mach 1 Mustang (ABOVE RIGHT) majored on its new styling, but the 351 Cleveland V8 under its hood also gave it very creditable performance on the street. The limited-production Torino Talledega (RIGHT) was a homologation special which allowed Ford to use the aerodynamically modified Torino in NASCAR events. Under the hood was the 428 Cobra Jet motor (LEFT), with 335bhp, although the racers had a great deal more power and performance.

For the street, of course, the cars had nothing more brutal than the 335bhp 428 motor. For racing, Ford furnished them with the new lightweight Boss 429 engine with its crescent-shaped combustion chambers (what Ford called the crescent shape was more commonly known as the "semi-hemi" design), although the new motor hadn't been homologated by the start of the NASCAR season and so the cars initially ran with the 427 wedge-head mill – homologated a couple of years earlier and still legal under NASCAR rules. The homologation run of 500 showroom cars was in fact achieved by putting the 429 into Mustangs rather than into Torino Talladegas, but NASCAR allowed this and the 429-powered Talladegas swept all before them when they finally did enter NASCAR races.

Mustangs were completely reworked for 1969, with longer and wider bodies. The restyle was undoubtedly an improvement, but the extra weight which came with it demanded drastic action if the cars were to remain competitive in the performance market. Ford took no chances, and announced the new Mach 1 model with the news that it had already taken no fewer than 295 speed records during September 1968 at Bonneville Salt Flats. With just 250bhp, the Mach 1's stock Cleveland 351 V8 didn't look like a winner, but it worked with other elements in the Mach 1 package to make a desirable street machine which sold well.

Until the end of the 1968 season, the real high-performance Mustangs had been the Shelby-developed machines, but not any more. The '69 Shelby Mustangs were slower than before, thanks both to the effects of emissions control gear on their engines and to the extra weight of the '69 bodies. They didn't sell well, either, and a lot of leftover '69s had to be modified for sale as 1970 models when the new season began.

There were still two models of Shelby Mustang on offer. The GT-350 now came with the new 351 Cleveland small-block V8 and 290bhp, although it could barely scrape under the 16-second barrier for the quarter-mile and its terminal speed of 89mph impressed nobody. The GT-500 – no longer a GT-500KR – could still manage respectable quarter-miles in less than 14 seconds with a terminal speed of 103mph, but enthusiasts complained that the advertised 355bhp were optimistic. Even so, the '69 Shelbys did look the part. Available in both fastback and

The 1969 Mach 1 Mustang had all the high-performance trappings, and the 428 Cobra Jet option fitted to this one made it live up to its appearance. The badging on the hood scoop (LEFT) showed that the 335bhp Ram-Air motor was fitted. Clever marketing made the Mach 1 very successful for 1969, although most had the tame 351 V8 with 350bhp or 390bhp. The very name (ABOVE) shouted "speed," and the hugely successful restyle (RIGHT) did the rest.

The new Mustang shell was also made available in Shelby guise for 1969 (OVERLEAF), but it promised more than it delivered. Power in this GT-500 model came from a 355bhp edition of the 428 Cobra Jet V8.

convertible forms, in both cases equipped with a rollover bar, they had longer noses than the standard cars and no fewer than five NACA-style ducts in their hood panels. Their tails were cut short and fitted with a lip spoiler and rear lights from a Mercury Cougar, and they had wide, reflective stripes running right along each side.

Enthusiasts who wanted a Mustang with grunt during the '69 season generally turned to one of the two limited-edition specials, however. Both were marketed under the Boss name, and both came about because of Ford's desire to do well in competition.

The Mustang Boss 429 came about because Ford had to homologate the 429 motor for the NASCAR Torino Talladegas. The Mustang's engine bay needed major surgery by a Ford sub-contractor before this massive motor

would fit, and the hood was equipped with a huge scoop to force-feed the four-barrel Holley carburetor with cool air. Fat tires and tough suspension completed the performance picture, but the Boss 429 also came with certain Mustang interior options as standard. In fact, it wasn't as fast on the street as its specification promised. The 375bhp semi-hemi motor powered the Mustang Boss 429 to respectable quarter-miles in the low 14s at 102-103mph, but on the street it couldn't match a Mach 1 Mustang fitted with the Cobra Jet 428 option.

The second Boss Mustang didn't arrive until April 1969, and was developed because Ford were tired of seeing Chevrolet's Z-28 Camaros walk all over the 289-powered Mustangs in the SCCA B-production series. Power came from a 302-cubic-inch small-block Windsor

V8, beefed up and fitted with modified heads from the 351 Cleveland big-block. The result gave excellent performance at high engine revolutions, which could be further improved by fitting the optional dual four-barrel carburetors.

Naturally, the Boss 302 had to be detuned for street use, and so Ford enhanced its appeal with the usual array of cosmetic tricks. Street versions – all based on the SportsRoof Mustang body – came with spoilers front and rear, side decals, hood stripes, blacked out grille and tail panel, and a mean-looking "shaker" air scoop protruding through the hood. All 1934 street versions built came with four-speed transmissions, stiffened suspension and front disk brakes.

However, neither street nor racing versions of the Boss 302 proved able to outrun the Z-28 Camaros they had been designed to beat. Quarter-miles in the high 14s at 96mph from the stock 289 motor were nothing startling, and Parnelli Jones couldn't beat the Penske and Donohue Z-28s in the Trans Am events, winning just four of the season's 12 races.

Over at Mercury division, the hot one for '69 was the Cyclone fastback, which was a twin brother of the Ford Torino. The entry-model, however, was a Cobra 428 equivalent, stripped out as far as Mercurys ever were and labelled as a Cyclone CJ. It was aimed at the Plymouth Road Runner market and came as standard with the 335bhp 428 big-block.

The search for aerodynamic advantage on the NASCAR ovals affected the Cyclone at mid-season, however. From January 1969 there was a companion Cyclone Spoiler model, with a huge aerofoil wing on its trunk which didn't actually have NASCAR approval. Standard in this was the 351 Windsor with 290bhp, although the 428 Cobra Jet option made it an altogether more exciting machine and offered quarter-miles at 101mph in just

under 14 seconds. There were two special-edition models of the Cyclone Spoiler, too, and these were known as the Dan Gurney Special and the Cale Yarborough Special. Both were named in honor of drivers who had been successful with NASCAR Mercurys.

Closer to the racing Cyclones, which had Boss 429 power, was the Cyclone Spoiler II. This arrived at mid-season, and picked up on the droop-snoot aerodynamics of the Dodge Charger 500 and Ford's Torino Talladega. Once again it had the trunk-lid spoiler for appearances' sake. Some street versions were built with the 429 motor, but just 370bhp were claimed for these.

At mid-season, Mercury also moved the Cougar into the high-performance market. Introduced in 1967 and sitting on a stretched Mustang platform, the Cougar had received only a lukewarm reception. For the latter part of '69, Mercury promoted it under the Cougar Eliminator name as a competitor in the Z-28 Camaro and Boss 302 Mustang market.

Despite a tempting array of engine options – 290bhp 351 Windsor, 290bhp Boss 302, 335bhp 428 Cobra Jet, and (according to some sources) 320bhp 390 and 370bhp 429 Semi-hemi – the Cougar Eliminator never quite delivered what it promised. Mostly, it was too heavy, laden down with the goodies expected on a Mercury; but it was also true that in street trim the larger engines like the 428 Cobra Jet were more than the chassis could comfortably handle. Experts claim that the Boss 302 engine option was the most satisfactory, although performance wasn't in the top division. Quarter-miles in the high 14s at a fraction over 96mph were not the stuff of which legends are made.

Nevertheless, the Cougar Eliminator did look good. Hood scoop, rear spoiler, and black stripe down the flanks all spelled performance in the '69 season. And on the street, it was a year when appearances counted.

Mercury had a lot more to say for themselves in 1969. Top right is the Cyclone CJ, based on the Ford Torino fastback and equipped with the 428 big-block V8. Side decals once again accentuated the high-performance look. The 428 motor (LEFT) pumped out 335bhp and was also found in the Cougar Eliminator (RIGHT), but Mercury's enlarged Mustang never quite lived up to its promises.

Dodge and Plymouth – aerodynamics

It wasn't a good year for Plymouth on the tracks. Star driver Richard Petty had a disappointing '68, wasn't impressed with what he saw coming along for '69, and asked if he could switch to the Dodge sister division and race the promising-looking Charger Daytona. Plymouth said no, so Petty promptly defected to Ford. Without Petty, and with poor aerodynamics in a field of cars with increasingly effective aerodynamics, Plymouth managed only two Grand National victories that season.

Dodge did very much better at NASCAR, though not as well as they'd hoped. Airflow work on the NASCAR Hemi Chargers helped a lot, but it wasn't until the super-aerodynamic Daytona Charger became available at the very end of the season that Dodge started winning convincingly. The new Charger came just a little too late, and the division had to be content with second place to Ford in the championships.

These differences between the divisions at NASCAR showed up on the street, too. Plymouth's high-performance image seemed to be on temporary hold, and at the beginning of the season Muscle Car enthusiasts were offered only a convertible Road Runner and a repackaged hot Barracuda which they couldn't have bought a year earlier. The Road Runner in fact appeared to have gone soft, picking up some luxury options for '69 which certainly weren't part of the original stripped-out performance package concept. Regular models came with the 383 motor and 335bhp as before, and the Hemi was again optional for competition use; there was also a wider choice of axle ratios than before, but it wasn't until mid-season that a really interesting new performance option arrived.

The new performance option was right in tune with the original Road Runner concept, because it offered maximum acceleration at low cost. Plymouth had

The bright color of this Plymouth GTX (RIGHT) was typical of the way Muscle Cars were going in the later 1960s. With 375bhp from its 440 V8, the car was fast but not among the fastest intermediates of its time. Much meaner-looking with its black paint job and red-striped tires was this 1969 Plymouth Road Runner (BELOW), although its 383 V8 with 335bhp made it a tad slower than the GTX. To boost '69 season sales, Plymouth added a six-barrel 440 to the Road Runner's options list, and finished the season with sales nearly twice their 1968 levels. The six-pack 440 could also be had in the GTX, and the red car overleaf has this performance option.

dropped the Super Commando 440 V8 into their budget Muscle Car, and had boosted its power to 390bhp by fitting three dual-barrel Holleys. The result was badged as a Road Runner 440+6, and with quarter-miles in the mid-13s, the car was very nearly as fast as a Hemi-powered Road Runner. Plymouth backed up the new motor with all the right goodies, making a Hurst shifter standard along with a lift-off fiberglass hood held down with NASCAR-style pins and finished in matt black.

Road Runner sales for '69 nearly doubled their '68 totals, but Barracuda production was down. Plymouth had tried hard, even at the beginning of the season: they had boosted the 383 V8's output to 330bhp, found room to fit power steering in the engine room, and built a cosmetic package around the Barracuda Formula S which they called the 'Cuda. The 'Cuda could be had with either the 275bhp 340 V8 or the 383, but the drawback was that it just wasn't fast enough. A stock 383 'Cuda took 15.5 seconds to run quarters, with a trap speed of only 92mph.

Recognizing the problem, Plymouth gave the model a mid-season shot in the arm by adding to the options list the triple-carburetor 440 from the Road Runner. The model wasn't a total success, though. Power steering had to be omitted once again for space reasons, no manual transmission could be had because the rear axle needed to be cushioned against the full torque of the 440, and the brakes weren't really up to the car's performance.

That left the GTX. Like the Road Runner, it had some inconsequential front and rear cosmetic changes for '69, a wider choice of axle ratios, and a Hurst shifter. Also new was the Air Grabber option, which consisted of dual air intakes in the hood with a dash-controlled shut-off. On the street, however, the GTX wasn't among the front runners, needing nearly seven seconds to reach 60mph from a standing-start. At the strips, the story was the same, and a 440-powered GTX ran quarter-miles in the mid-14s at well under 100mph. Serious performance buyers ordered their GTXs with Hemi power, but their numbers weren't enough to make much difference to sales, which were down to just over 15,600 from last season's 19,000.

The Dodge Daytona (RIGHT AND
BELOW) was undoubtedly one of
the wildest looking Muscle Cars
ever. The bullet nose and aerofoil
tail had been developed to improve
its performance in high-speed
NASCAR racing, but they made the
car look fast even when it was
standing still and certainly made it
stand out in the parking lot. For
those reasons, they had great
appeal to the street fraternity; at all
practicable speeds, though, they
made no difference whatsoever.

The Hemi – or King Kong as it was familiarly known – was still very much around in 1969, and could be had in a variety of models from Dodge and Plymouth. The motor itself, seen on the right in a Dodge Super Bee, was still good for 425bhp, still had an orange-painted block, and was still mostly ordered for competition use because the performance it offered just wasn't necessary for everyday driving. The Coronet-derived Super Bee (LEFT) looked mean, but there was no easy way of telling that this one had Hemi power. Nor was it obvious that the blue Charger (BELOW) was running a Hemi, although its no-frills appearance did hint that the buyer had spent his money on something other than cosmetic options.

The hot Dodges for '69 were once again grouped together as the Scat Pack for marketing purposes, and this year they had a single broad tail-stripe flanked by a pair of thinner stripes instead of last year's twin stripes. They came as Chargers, Coronets, and Darts, just as in '68, although there were plenty of changes.

Most memorable of them all was undoubtedly the Charger Daytona, the bullet-nosed, winged monster designed for the superspeedways and released to the public purely for homologation purposes. But Dodge didn't have that car ready until late in the season. They started at NASCAR with racing versions of the Charger 500, made more aerodynamic than last year's models by means of a flush grille and backlight. Other Charger models didn't have these changes, which were added to leftover '68 shells by a Michigan custom shop and also appeared on the street Charger 500. Competition Charger 500s had Hemi power, and could storm to 109mph quarter-miles in the mid-13s. For the street, however, the 375bhp 440 Magnum V8 was standard.

When Ford Torino Talladegas and Mercury Cyclones proved too quick for the Hemi Chargers at high speeds, Dodge answered with the aerodynamically-improved Charger Daytona, which was announced in mid-April 1969. To improve airflow, the car had a bullet-shaped nose-cone added to its existing body panels, and to minimize lift at maximum speeds on the tracks there was a chin spoiler at the front and a huge adjustable aerofoil mounted on twin tailplanes above the trunk. The result was an improvement of some 20 percent in airflow at very high speeds – enough to make the Charger Daytona convincingly faster than the Fords and Mercurys.

The '69 Dodge Coronet R/T 440 (LEFT) had a pair of mean-looking induction scoops on its hood to feed fresh air to its motor.

That year's Oldsmobile 4-4-2 didn't offer much which the '68s hadn't, although the car still looked tough even in basic trim like the one pictured (RIGHT). Inside the 4-4-2 (BELOW), there wasn't much to suggest that this was intended to be a high-performance car. The floor shift gave a hint, but the air conditioner fitted to this example wasn't what Muscle Cars had been all about in the early days.

While these aerodynamic addenda made absolutely no difference to performance at any legal speed on the street, and also added enough weight to make a Charger Daytona slower than a regular Charger 500 at the strip, they did make a powerful statement about the car's performance potential even when it was standing still. Street fans loved them, and the 505 Charger Daytonas made to meet the NASCAR homologation rules were snapped up quickly, despite their enormous cost.

Top-seller among the hot Coronets was the Super Bee, marketed as a separate model. It was pretty well unchanged from its 1968 incarnation, although it followed the Road Runner in adding a two-door hardtop body to the original pillared coupé style. The 335bhp 383 remained standard and, once again like the Road Runner, a 390bhp 440 engine with three two-barrel carburetors was introduced as an option at mid-season. Dodge called it the 440 Six-Pack, and sold just over 1900 of them before the season ended. With quarter-miles in the mid-13s at 105mph, this was a very serious challenger at the strips.

Both Super Bee and R/T 440 derivatives of the Coronet could be bought with Hemi power, although the standard R/T 440 differed from 1968's model only in its adoption of the Ramcharger fresh-air induction package with twin hood scoops. The R/T 440 had had its day, however. Production dropped for '69, while sales of the Super Bee soared to nearly 28,000.

The Dart was still around, of course, still with the 340 or 383 V8s in GTS form. Around 600 were equipped with the 440 Magnum V8 for competition use, but by far the most significant development in the Dart range was the arrival of the new Swinger model. Top option was the Swinger 340, a lightweight base-model Dart hardtop with the 275bhp 340 V8. Performance was not really up to Muscle Car standards, but Dodge included the Swinger 340 in its Scat Pack, emphasizing the car's appeal to young buyers who wanted cars with a performance image.

Buick, Oldsmobile, and Pontiac

Oldsmobile's 4-4-2 didn't do so well during '69, and end-of-season figures showed a downturn in sales. One reason, undoubtedly, was that the '69 model didn't offer very much which the '68 hadn't had. Bolder graphics and cosmetic changes front and rear weren't really enough on their own.

That didn't make the '69 4-4-2 a bad car in any way, of course. The most popular body style remained the Holiday hardtop coupé, and the top performance option remained the W-30 package, which included the 360bhp Force-Air 400 option also available separately. The entry-level 4-4-2 still had its 350bhp 400 V8, although new for '69 was the W-32 package, which brought 350bhp with automatic transmission in place of the detuned 325bhp motor offered in '68. On the street, a W-30 could still streak to 60mph in a little more than six seconds, and at the strip it could return quarter-miles in the low 13s with trap speeds of over 103mph. As a performer, this car was still in the first division.

The 1969 Oldsmobile 4-4-2 looked especially good as a convertible, and the white decals on the hood of this red example (ABOVE LEFT) give just the right visual impression. Only one in six 4-4-2s for '69 came with this body style, though. The 400-cubic-inch V8 in the 4-4-2 (BELOW FAR LEFT) came in three different states of tune, starting at 325bhp and running up to 360bhp.

Pontiac meanwhile had a facelifted Firebird, which looked rather more stylish as a convertible (ABOVE) than as a coupé (BELOW LEFT). Base engines were in-line sixes, but the top Firebird option was a Ram-Air 400 V8 with 345bhp.

The Hurst/Olds 4-4-2 remained available, too, with its 455-cubic-inch motor slightly down on power as a result of emissions control equipment. Torque was still massive enough to give sub-six-second times for the 0 to 60 test which mattered on the street, however, and quarter-miles in the high 13s at around 101mph kept the car competitive at the strips. Dual air scoops in the hood, a rear spoiler, and Firefrost Gold paint gave the car the visual appeal which Muscle fans were now demanding, and this model at least recorded an upturn in sales – 914 as against 515 in '68.

Buick's sole Muscle Car remained the GS-400, this year tricked out with new body side graphics, altered front and rear details, and a subtle twin-entry hood scoop. In standard 340bhp form, it remained a good street machine with 0 to 60mph times of just over six seconds, but performance tailed off at higher engine revolutions and the car needed almost 16 seconds for a quarter-mile with a terminal speed of 89-90mph.

More performance could be had from '69's new options, though. The Stage I package matched a 350bhp motor with oversize exhausts to a limited-slip differential and a lowered axle ratio, and the Stage II package boosted power to 360bhp. Optional on all the GS-400s were a heavy-duty Rallye suspension and front disk brakes, which came with power assistance.

Over at Pontiac, 1969 saw a pair of new high-performance sub-series of existing models. From the Firebird line came the Firebird Trans Am, while the GTO Judge introduced a stripped-out version of Pontiac's best-selling intermediate to the budget muscle market created by the Plymouth Road Runner.

Like the Camaro on which it was based, the Firebird was longer, wider, and heavier for 1969. Serious performance versions started with the Firebird 400, with 330bhp under its hood, and buyers could go on up to 335bhp with

Most interesting of the 1969 Firebirds was the new Trans Am model (THESE PAGES), dressed to kill with blue racing stripes on its white bodywork. This year was the only one when a convertible Trans Am would be available alongside the more popular hardtop coupé. All types came with the Ram Air 400 motor, although there were two different states of tune. The engine pictured below left has the top-option Ram Air IV, with 345bhp and 430lbf ft of torque. The foam surround helped funnel the air collected by the hood scoops into the induction system.

That something was to introduce the Trans Am appearance package in March 1969. Firebirds had of course been racing in the Trans Am series, although they had used Chevrolet 302 motors from the Z-28 Camaro in order to get under the 305-cubic-inch ceiling. And Pontiac engineers were working on a new 303 V8, a short-stroke derivative of the 400, which did appear in Firebirds in some NASCAR races late in the season. Production problems meant that this engine never reached the show-rooms, however, and so the buyers had to settle for a Firebird Trans Am with the 335bhp Ram Air III 400 as standard or the 345bhp Ram Air IV version as an option.

If the Firebird Trans Am didn't offer any more performance than a well-optioned regular Firebird, it nevertheless had enormous street appeal. The car looked superb with its blue racing stripes on its white body, a twin-scoop hood, air extractors behind the front wheelarches, and a rear aerofoil. Special power steering and power brakes with lowered levels of assistance also gave a more sporting feel to the cars, and Trans Am buyers were at least rewarded with a Firebird which was enjoyable to drive.

Like the Firebird, the GTO picked up new engine options for 1969, although all versions of the 400 which Pontiac offered for their intermediate star were more powerful than those in the ponycar. The entry-level motor was a 350bhp edition of the 400; last year's 400 HO had gone in favor of a 366bhp Ram Air III motor; and for serious performance there was the 370bhp Ram Air IV, which came as a package with a lowered rear axle ratio and other performance goodies.

the Ram Air III option which replaced last season's 400 HO, and later to 345bhp with the Ram Air IV option which replaced Ram Air III. With that option, a Firebird would take just over 14 seconds to run the quarter-mile, with a trap speed of 101mph. However, Firebird sales were down on '68, and Pontiac managers reasoned that they needed to do something fast.

However, neither these improved performance options nor the minor interior and exterior cosmetic changes to the GTO were 1969's real news. That was a stripped-out, Road Runner-style GTO known as the GTO Judge, which was announced in December 1968. As it was an extra-cost option on the GTO line, it couldn't compete with the Road Runner on price, but it was remarkably good value for money, all the same.

Pontiac aimed the GTO Judge very carefully at its target market of young performance enthusiasts. Bright colors, side decals, hood scoops, a blacked-out grille, and rear spoiler gave all the right visual messages, and even the name was calculated to have a special appeal. It came from the TV comedy programme, *Rowan and Martin's Laugh-In*, where it was an irreverent name for a pompous and authoritarian figure. The GTO Judge was anything but pompous and authoritarian – but the reverse-humor and the association with the popular program worked.

Besides, the GTO Judge wasn't just an appearance package; it also had performance appeal. Its hood scoops were functional, feeding cold air to the standard 366bhp Ram Air III motor or to an optional 370bhp Ram Air IV. On the street and at the strips it offered just the right level of performance to appeal to speed-crazy youngsters whose pockets weren't as deep as their desires. Sad to tell, however, it didn't stop GTO sales from sliding in '69.

Chevrolet

For 1969, Chevrolet continued to rely on their long-serving 396 as the primary muscle motor in Novas, Chevelles, and Camaros, all with the SS tag. From September 1969 (when Chevies were still officially '69 models because the GM strike had held up introduction of the 1970 cars), a bigger bore introduced to help the engine

Pontiac's GTO (BELOW) for 1969 didn't look all that different to the previous year's edition, although there were some improved performance packages. Instead, the division had concentrated on developing the GTO Judge (RIGHT) to combat Plymouth's Road Runner in the budget-muscle market. In essence, it was a stripped-out GTO with paint, decals and other addenda carefully calculated to appeal to younger and less wealthy performance enthusiasts. The Judge soon acquired a rather tacky image, but it made its mark on the Muscle Car scene.

Meanwhile, Chevrolet's entrant in the budget-muscle stakes was the Nova SS (BELOW RIGHT), which certainly looked the part with its smart black paint job, dual hood scoops, and raised-letter tires. The engine was a 402-cubic-inch V8, although Chevy referred to it as a 396 – the capacity of the well-respected engine from which it was derived.

meet emissions control regulations put the actual capacity up to 402 cubic inches, but the engine was still referred to as a 396. The 427 also appeared in a few competition Chevelles and Camaros, as well as seeing its last season of production in the full-size Impala SS. And the 302 remained available in the Z-28 Camaros, which once again won the Trans Am series in the hands of Mark Donohue.

This year, Chevrolet looked on the Nova SS as its budget-muscle competitor for the Road Runner market. More than 7000 were built, although the 375bhp L-78 option (which wasn't advertised) proved much more popular than the standard 350bhp offering, which this year had a strengthened block and a small power increase from 295bhp to 300bhp. Quarter-miles at 14 seconds and 100mph were more than acceptable for a car of its price.

Next up in price came the Camaros, restyled for this season with slimmer body contours, lower wheelarches with horizontal "brows," a vee grille, and a revised tail end. Twin hood bulges and an optional lip spoiler at the tail were dictated more by fashion than performance, and the power options remained as they had been for 1968: 325bhp, 350bhp, and 375bhp 396s.

The top-performing production Camaros were once again Z-28s, however, still with the 302-cubic-inch V8, which this year was made more durable thanks to four-bolt main bearing caps. Its 290 advertised horses were still way short of the real figure, but even the Z-28 was eclipsed by a pair of limited-production hot Camaros.

Not long after the Camaro had appeared on the scene, a small number of Chevrolet dealers, such as Baldwin-Motion, had started offering converted cars with the big

Hot Camaros for '69: the main picture shows the formidable 427-powered Yenko Camaro, while above are the Z-28 model and its 302-cubic-inch motor.

The demand for performance was still strong enough in 1969 for Chevrolet to squeeze oversize motors into some models and to build limited runs of them. Dealer Don Yenko persuaded them to fit the big 427 into Camaros (LEFT), and he was also behind the competition-special Chevelle with the same big-block motor (BELOW RIGHT). The Copo Camaro (BELOW) also had the 427 motor in a mean-looking package. But these were specialist cars, and for most people the Chevelle SS 396 (RIGHT) was fast enough. Its facelift also made it a particularly attractive piece of machinery.

427 V8. The most famous was Don Yenko, a Pennsylvania dealer, and for 1969 he succeeded in persuading the factory to build a run of 201 "Yenko Camaros" with the iron-block L-72 427 motor. The factory claimed 425bhp; Yenko claimed 450 for those he sold; but whatever the truth was, even the Yenko Camaro couldn't touch the ultimate '69s from the factory. These were a limited run of 50 dragstrip specials, with the 430bhp ZL-1 aluminum-block Corvette 427 engine, equipped with three two-barrel carburetors. For street enthusiasts, cars like these might just as well never have existed, however, because they couldn't get their hands on one.

As the Impala SS with its 427 really wasn't in the Muscle Car league any more, the biggest high-performance Chevrolets for '69 were Chevelles. This year brought a facelift for the 112-inch wheelbase intermediate, but the 325bhp, 350bhp, and 375bhp options for the SS 396 became an option package on Chevelle and Malibu Sport Coupés and on Malibu convertibles, instead of a separate series. It could also be had on the new Chevelle 300 pillared coupé. Special customers were able to buy one of about 500 cars with the L-72 iron-block 427 and 425bhp, but these were competition machines and didn't appear on the street.

AMC – trying even harder

Encouraged by the success of their AMX two-seater coupé during its half-season in '68, AMC aimed even higher for '69. Sales unfortunately didn't match expectations, but the car was still a formidable machine with its top-option 315bhp 390 V8. Most important of the few changes which AMC did make for the new season was the Hurst shifter, which erased the '68 models' biggest failing.

AMC also used Hurst to assemble a run of 50 Super Stock AMX coupés for NHRA competition. The factory claimed 340bhp for the 390 engine in these, which had a raised compression ratio, a pair of Holley carburetors, competition headers and exhausts, and a few other tweaks performed by Hurst; however, the NHRA rated the motor at 420bhp, which was a lot nearer to its true output. With all this power, the little coupés were enormously fast, and the best quarter-mile recorded by one that year was 10.73 seconds at 128mph.

Appearance mattered, even in a car designed exclusively for the dragstrip, and the Super Stock AMX cars were mostly painted in an eyecatching red, white, and blue color scheme. Loud paint was also part of the Big Bad option package which AMC offered on street cars from the spring of 1969, and the body-color bumpers, spoilers and other visual gimmicks which made up the rest of this option demonstrated that AMC had understood perfectly what performance fans wanted that year.

The alliance with Hurst bore further fruit in the shape of the astonishing AMC/Hurst SC/Rambler, more commonly known as the Scrambler and introduced at midyear. At its heart was a 106-inch-wheelbase Rambler Rogue hardtop – a model which was in its final year of production. The Scrambler helped it to go out in a blaze of glory. AMC planned to build 500, but the car proved such a success that over 1500 were eventually made in 1969.

Under the hood of the Scrambler was the 315bhp 390 V8 from the AMX with a straight-through dual exhaust system, and this drove a limited-slip Twin-Grip differential through a four-speed Borg Warner automatic transmission with a Hurst shifter. Quarter-miles were in the low 14s at over 100mph, and a Scrambler could reach 60mph from a standing start in 6.3 seconds – well up with the street's fastest for that year. Heavy-duty suspension and front disk brakes ensured that the car handled and stopped well, and there wasn't any doubt about its street appeal. The Scrambler had another of AMC's eyecatching red, white, and blue color schemes, this time with striped headrests as well, and a canted fiberglass hood scoop quite unlike those seen on other makes in 1969. It was barely recognizable as a derivative of the staid Rambler, long seen as an elderly driver's car.

AMC's 1969 offerings were very tempting indeed. The AMX 390 looked good (LEFT) and went well thanks to its 390-cubic-inch V8 (RIGHT), while the Scrambler (BELOW RIGHT) used the same motor, a time-expired compact sedan body, and a striking paint job to produce one of the year's most desirable Muscle Cars.

Muscle Car Choice – 1969

Subcompacts
AMC AMX 390

Compacts
AMC-Hurst SC/Rambler
Chevrolet Nova SS 396
Dodge Dart GTS

Ponycars
Chevrolet Camaro SS 396
Chevrolet Camaro Z-28
Ford Mustang Boss 302
Ford Mustang Boss 429
Mercury Cougar
Eliminator
Plymouth Barracuda
(with 383 option)
Pontiac Firebird
(with 400 option)
Pontiac Firebird Trans Am
Shelby Mustang GT-350
Shelby Mustang GT-500

Intermediates
Buick GS-400
Chevrolet Chevelle SS 396
Dodge Charger 500
Dodge Charger Daytona
Dodge Coronet R/T
Dodge Coronet Super Bee
Ford Fairlane Cobra 428
Ford Torino Talladega
Mercury Cyclone
Mercury Cyclone Spoiler
Mercury Cyclone Spoiler II
Oldsmobile 4-4-2
Plymouth GTX
Plymouth Road Runner
Pontiac GTO
Pontiac GTO Judge

1970

Over the Hill

By 1970, America's love-affair with the Muscle Car had begun to cool. The market was flooded with a vast array of different models, all vying for a piece of the sales action, but the sales peak had passed. One reason, of course, was that overall new-car sales in the U.S. declined in 1970, by some 11 percent. But sales of Muscle Cars were hit harder than most.

It isn't hard to see why this should have been so. The emphasis had already begun to drift away from outright performance to outrageous appearance, and the motor manufacturers had already discovered that the right paint scheme and graphics would do more for sales than a dozen extra brake horsepower. Those extra brake horsepower were in any case becoming harder to find, as tightening emissions controls forced compression ratios down and fuel consumption up. General Motors was obliged to raise the 400-cubic-inch engine size limit it had imposed on its intermediates to 455 cubic inches; without that,

performance losses would have been far too noticeable.

Young buyers were also faced with a serious problem. It was becoming more and more expensive to insure a Muscle Car, as the insurance companies recognized that the combination of a young inexperienced driver and a high-performance car was likely to be a bad risk. The question of automotive safety had also become a public preoccupation, and public opinion was turning against high-performance cars by 1970. As a result, fewer and fewer buyers actually wanted a Muscle Car.

Almost all the Muscle Car lines fared badly during 1970, and even the hugely popular Plymouth Road Runner ended the season some 50 percent down on its 1969 sales total. There were success stories, of course, new models from Dodge and Plymouth among them – but the overall picture was a gloomy one. All the major manufacturers pulled out of Trans Am racing at the end of the 1970 season, recognizing that expenditure on factory-backed racing programs was no longer justified by increased sales.

For all that, the 1970 crop of Muscle Cars included some of the best examples of the kind. Now that braking and suspension were at last matching the awesome acceleration available from the most powerful engines, the best Muscle Cars offered well-balanced packages. Sadly for performance fans, things would get worse rather than better for 1971.

Dodge and Plymouth – something old, something new

The MOPAR Muscle Cars continued to have a high marketing profile for 1970. Dodge still had their Scat Pack with bumble-bee tail stripes, and Plymouth now joined in with their Rapid Transport System. At NASCAR, Plymouths were in the ascendant over the Dodges, but the MOPAR Trans Am campaign wasn't so successful in spite of the all-new models it was designed to promote.

Plymouth's image-leader for 1970 was undoubtedly the Road Runner Superbird, a NASCAR homologation special which was a close cousin to Dodge's 1969 Charger Daytona. The Plymouth was based on the restyled 1970 Road Runner, modified with a bullet-shaped nose cone and huge rear "tailplane" aerofoil which both followed the same lines as the Charger Daytona but were different in detail. The NASCAR cars were Hemi-powered, and were capable of more than 220mph; driver Pete Hamilton

The Dodge Challenger, new for 1970, was developed alongside the Plymouth Barracuda but was nevertheless slightly larger. Bold paint, a matt black hood with air scoop, and side decals made this 340 model look as fast as it went.

achieved a near 150mph *average* to win the Daytona 500 in a Superbird this year. Hemis were also optional for the street version, although most street machines had one of the two versions of the 440 Super Commando V8.

NASCAR had changed its homologation rules for 1970, so Plymouth had to build 1000 Superbirds for sale to the public whereas Dodge had been obliged to build just 500 Charger Daytonas in 1969. In fact, the division managed to ship 1920 examples, which rather gives the lie to stories that they were next to unsaleable. Stock street drivetrain was the 375bhp four-barrel 440 V8 with a Torque Flite automatic transmission, but the 390bhp 440 Six-Pack was optional, as was a four-speed manual transmission. Weight counted against the Superbird in quarter-mile events, as it had with the similar Charger Daytona, but with the 375bhp motor it could manage quarter-miles in the low 14s at 103mph; Hemi-powered examples brought these down into the mid-13s.

The regular Road Runner was distinguished from last season's offering by a restyle which added dummy air

Plymouth's Road Runner remained a strong seller in 1970, and the example pictured on the right has the optional 440 Six-Pack motor. The fat tires and the matt black hood with its huge air scoop add greatly to its aggressive looks. The NASCAR Road Runners, however, were modified in much the same way as the NASCAR Dodges: they had bullet-shaped noses and large rear aerofoils, and these components were homologated on a limited production run sold through Plymouth dealers and called the Road Runner Superbird (MAIN PICTURE). Onlookers whose attention had been grabbed by the car's outrageous appearance could hardly fail to notice who had built it before they looked away (LEFT)!

There was a third engine option for the Road Runner in 1970: alongside the regular 383 and the 440 Six-Pack, Plymouth offered the Hemi (RIGHT). As usual, it was the least commonly specified of the options, and as usual, it wasn't immediately obvious by looking at the car (LEFT) that the mighty 426 was under the hood. Nevertheless, that paint and decal job and those fat tires should have been warning enough.

For the budget-muscle market, Plymouth fielded the Duster 340, a compact coupé with loud paint jobs (BELOW LEFT) and 275bhp-worth of V8 under its hood (BELOW).

scoops in the rear fender and smarter front and rear details. Once again, the entry-level motor was a 335bhp 383; next up was the 440-6 with 390bhp; and the faithful Hemi was still around for those who wanted maximum performance. Even this old warrior had been modified in the interests of exhaust emissions control, and for this year its solid lifters were replaced by hydraulic items which were said to help the engine meet the latest clean air standards. Power output was still quoted conservatively at 425bhp, though whether there had been any loss from the real output is debatable.

The GTX of course still figured in the line-up, too, with new smoother lines but now without a convertible option. Buyers could choose from a 440 with the same advertised power and torque figures as last year (despite a lower compression ratio); the 390bhp 440-6; and the latest hydraulic-lifter Hemi. Optional with the 440-6

motor, and standard with the Hemi, was the latest version of the Air Grabber hood vent, now consisting of a single flap which could be raised and lowered from inside the car. It was typical of the times that the sides of the raised vent featured a shark decal, presumably designed to strike terror into challengers on the street. Several axle ratios could be had to turn the GTX into a hot performer, but of course it was always heavier than a Road Runner and therefore never quite as fast.

The hot Plymouths for 1970 were getting smaller, though, even if the Rapid Transit System did embrace one full-size model – the Sport Fury GT with a 440 Super Commando V8. This year, the division introduced not one, but two new models on 108-inch wheelbases.

Many Muscle Car fans would agree that the more exciting newcomer was the Duster. Entry-level models didn't have the power and performance to qualify as muscle machinery, but the top-option Duster 340 was capable of quarter-miles in the mid-13s at 107mph with the right combination of axle and transmission options.

The Duster was based on the Valiant sedan, but had been given a pretty fastback coupé body which was light enough to allow supercar performance from the 275bhp 340 V8 in the top model. Plymouth had seen the car as an equivalent of the Dodge Dart Swinger 340, but the Duster was in fact rather better. Graphics, paint, and smart interior design helped the Duster to become a winner in the budget-muscle market and, in its way, the Duster 340 was as much of a triumph for Plymouth as the original Road Runner had been two years earlier. High sales of the whole Duster range during the 1970 season demonstrated that Plymouth had hit the bullseye in other areas of the Muscle Car market, too.

The Duster's success might have been something of a surprise to those used to big-engined intermediate Muscle Cars. However, the success of the third-generation Barracuda range, introduced in 1970, was rather more predictable. Plymouth stuck to a 108-inch wheelbase for their new, unit-construction ponycar range, which now came only in notchback or convertible forms and no longer included fastback variants. Lower and wider than before, the 1970 models were the neatest looking Barracudas yet.

This year, the performance models were all called 'Cudas. A 335bhp 383 was the basic powerpack, although a cheaper version with the 275bhp 340 V8 was optional. Going on up through the range, 'Cuda buyers could order the 375bhp 440, the 390bhp 440-6, and of course the 425bhp Hemi. Axle ratios came in a vast array of options, and with the right combination it was possible to get quarters in the mid-14s at 98mph from a 383-engined 'Cuda, low 14s at 100mph from a 440-6, and mid-13s at 108mph with what enthusiasts quickly named the Hemi 'Cuda. Dual hood scoops on all 'Cudas were for looks only, but it was possible to order the 383 and the two 440s with a shaker scoop, which came as standard with the Hemi.

Plymouth were keen to attract maximum publicity for their new ponycars, and the obvious method was through a Trans Am entry. The Trans Am cars were prepared by Dan Gurney's All-American Racers, and had a special short-stroke edition of the 340 V8 which displaced 305 cubic inches and was thus just within the capacity limit set by the SCCA. Naturally, there had to be a homologation run of Trans Am 'Cudas – and so there was, although they differed quite considerably from the actual race cars.

Plymouth couldn't call them Trans Am models, because Pontiac had already put that name on to their hot Firebird. Instead, they called them AAR 'Cudas, the initials standing for All-American Racers. Introduced in March 1970, the AAR 'Cudas wore American flag decals behind distinctive strobe-style, bodyside stripes, and their matt black fiberglass hoods were pinned down, NASCAR-style. These 'Cudas were among the first production cars to have fatter tires at the rear than at the front (which improved their handling in turns), and their tail ends were jacked-up to clear these tires, so giving a raked appearance which had immense street appeal. This was set off by side exit exhausts which emerged just ahead of the rear wheels, and made exactly the right noises for the street crowd.

The street AAR 'Cudas didn't have the Trans Am 305 motor, however. Instead, they had an upgraded 340 V8

Loud paint again on this 1970 Plymouth 'Cuda ragtop (ABOVE LEFT), which is fitted with the 440 Super Commando V8 and the optional "shaker" hood scoop. The yellow hardtop (RIGHT) has the Hemi option, which always came with a shaker scoop. The engine bay picture of this car (ABOVE RIGHT) shows how the feature got its name: attached directly to the engine and protruding through a cutout in the hood panel, the scoop shook along with the engine.

with the triple two-barrel carburetor set-up from the 440-6. Plymouth claimed that this put out 290bhp, but it most probably had nearer 350bhp. Even so, the AAR 'Cuda wasn't enormously fast at the strips, relying instead on its visual appeal for sales. Nor did the 305-engined car prove very successful on the tracks, where driver Swede Savage could not outrun the Boss 302 Mustangs and Z-28 Camaros in the Trans Am series.

Dodge, too, ran a new model in 1970 Trans Am events. Developed alongside the new Barracuda, the Dodge nevertheless ended up with a longer 110-inch wheelbase after the division had decided to tackle the more affluent end of the ponycar market which was then dominated by the Mercury Cougar. Trans Am success eluded Dodge's new Challenger and driver Sam Posey in the same way as it eluded Plymouth's new 'Cuda, but the range sold very well through the showrooms.

The racing Challengers had the 440bhp, short-stroke 305 motor, but the homologation cars for the street which appeared at mid-year were equipped with the same triple-carb 340 as the street AAR 'Cudas. What Dodge called the Challenger T/A (for Trans Am) borrowed a number of other cues from the AAR 'Cuda, too, with fat

rear tires and a jacked-up rear end, side-exit exhausts, a pinned-down fiberglass hood in matt black with a huge air scoop, a trunk lid spoiler, and side stripes. On the street, a Challenger T/A impressed with its sub-six-second 0 to 60mph times, but at the drag strips, owners had to be content with quarter-mile times in the mid-14s at under 100mph.

Plymouth's Trans Am contender was a destroked 340 'Cuda, but the homologation cars had the regular 340 motor, pepped up by a three-carburetor six-pack set-up. The green AAR 'Cuda (ABOVE LEFT) shows the matt black hood and decals special to the model, with the AAR badge just visible on the rear fender. The AAR 'Cuda and the Dodge Challenger T/A were the only models ever to be offered with this six-barrel edition of the 340 V8 (LEFT). The triple-carburetor package is seen to good advantage in a Challenger (RIGHT), with air cleaner removed. The jacked-up rear end and side-exit exhausts mark out the red car (ABOVE RIGHT) as a Challenger T/A.

The Challenger T/A was of course made in only limited numbers, and most performance fans who wanted a Challenger during 1970 settled for the Challenger R/T. This didn't have the fat rear tires, jacked-up rear, or side-exit exhausts of the T/A, although it could be bought with more powerful engines and was therefore ultimately a faster car. The 335bhp 383 was for starters; the 440 Magnum in 375bhp or 390bhp Six-Pack forms was next up; and racers could order a Hemi Challenger which would streak to 60mph in well under six seconds and would turn quarter-miles in 14 seconds at 104mph. The 440 Six-Pack also offered formidable performance, taking a full six seconds for the 0 to 60mph sprint but achieving quarter-miles in the mid-13s. It all went to prove that the limited-edition model wasn't always the best performer.

At NASCAR events during 1970, Dodge campaigned the Charger Daytonas which had been homolgated at the end of the '69 season, although they were bettered by the Plymouth Superbirds. The Charger Daytona was no longer available through the showrooms, and Charger fans were offered only a Charger R/T with the 335bhp 383 motor or a Charger 500 which had lost its flush grille and backlight and was not as fast as the '69 cars. Even so, the 440 Magnum in 375bhp or optional 390bhp Six-Pack forms meant that this was no slouch on the street.

Coronet sales nose-dived during 1970, despite new styling with a split grille and decorative side scoops on the rear fenders. The R/T came with the 375bhp 440 Magnum, and a handful were Hemi-powered. This year wasn't a good one for the Coronet-derived Super Bee, either, which came as usual with the 383, the 440 Six-Pack or – rarely – the Hemi. And further down the scale,

Looking quite different from the T/A on the previous page is this Challenger R/T (RIGHT), equipped with the regular 383 V8.

The main picture shows a 1970 Charger with all the goodies: the car is an R/T SE model with Hemi power. The SE designation stood for Special Edition, and brought with it a vinyl roof and smaller backlight, among other items.

Overleaf is one of 1970's Scat Pack, a Coronet-based Super Bee from Dodge. The 383 was standard, but 440 Six-Pack and Hemi options were also available. The tail spoiler, which aped the huge wing on Dodge's Charger Daytona, was purely for looks.

Dodge had abandoned the Dart GTS 383, leaving the Swinger 340 as the quickest of the Dart family. Despite bumble-bee stripes around the tail which identified it as a member of 1970's Scat Pack, it couldn't achieve the levels of performance offered elsewhere.

Buick, Oldsmobile, Pontiac – the 455s

When GM raised the capacity limit on intermediates for 1970, Pontiac and Oldsmobile already had 455-cubic-inch motors available in the other models. Buick, however, were obliged to develop a fresh engine for their GS muscle model, and in many ways the Buick 455 was the best of the bunch. It was the largest V8 engine the division had ever produced, and was plenty powerful enough, not only for the Muscle Cars, but for the larger and heavier Buicks into which it also found it way.

The Buick 455's strength lay in its tremendous torque, which peaked at 510lbf ft at a low 2800rpm. Regular versions had 350bhp; Stage I types added a high-lift camshaft, bigger valves, and a higher compression ratio to give 360bhp. These motors went into Buick's restyled GS models, sitting on the same 112-inch wheelbase as last year but featuring new and visually better-balanced sheet metal which added a couple of inches to their overall length. With the Stage I package came a Positraction rear end, and a GS-455 equipped with this option was good for quarter-miles in the mid-13s at 105mph. That was impressive, but the car was not to be messed with on

The 440 Six-Pack option fitted to this Dodge Charger hardtop (LEFT) brought 390bhp, but the single-carburetor 440 Magnum, seen (RIGHT) in a Super Bee, had just 375bhp – still enough to see off a lot of the opposition.

Buick's newly restyled GS is seen here in ragtop form (ABOVE), with the 360bhp Stage I edition of the new 455 motor. Enormous torque made these Buicks accelerate very quickly indeed.

Convertible versions of the 1970 Buick Gran Sport were quite rare (LEFT AND RIGHT). All of them came with the new 455-big-block motor, which in the cars pictured had the Stage I performance option. The hood scoops were functional, as the air collectors on top of this Stage I motor (BELOW LEFT) show.

The dual hood scoops on this 1970 Oldsmobile 4-4-2 (BELOW RIGHT) gave the car an aggressive appearance, and the 455 V8 provided very good performance. But the car was too heavy to rank among the leaders.

the street, either. Zero to 60mph standing starts of just 5.5 seconds were easily enough to frighten away most challengers.

The 400-cubic-inch motor had of course been dropped, although the entry-level 350 V8 remained available in what was now simply known as the Buick GS. At mid-year, Buick hoped to give sales a boost with the new GSX model, a GS-455 Sport Coupé with added visual appeal in the shape of special graphics, aerodynamic addenda, and a hood-mounted tacho. These cars came with uprated suspension, and most had the Stage I 455 motor, but they weren't enough to stop the sales slide.

Production dropped for Oldsmobile's 4-4-2 in 1970, too. This year, the venerable model-line was freshened up with a few cosmetic changes, and the 455 V8 from last year's Hurst/Olds model was standardized. It came with 365bhp and a single four-barrel carburetor as standard, or as part of the W-30 package with air induction and other goodies for 370bhp. More streetable was the W-32 package, which offered a slightly detuned W-30 motor. In full 370bhp tune, a 1970 W-30 4-4-2 was probably quicker on the street than any other model to bear its name, and offered 60mph in just 5.7 seconds from a standing-start. At the strip, though, quarter-miles in the mid-14s didn't put the car up among that year's leaders.

The 1970 Pontiac GTO had a distinctive and attractive new front end made of Endura, and there were pronounced flares over its wheelarches (BELOW). The GTO Judge (LEFT AND RIGHT) was still on offer, still with loud paint schemes, and this year with trick decals which some observers thought rubbed shoulders with bad taste. It sold well enough, but not as well as in 1969.

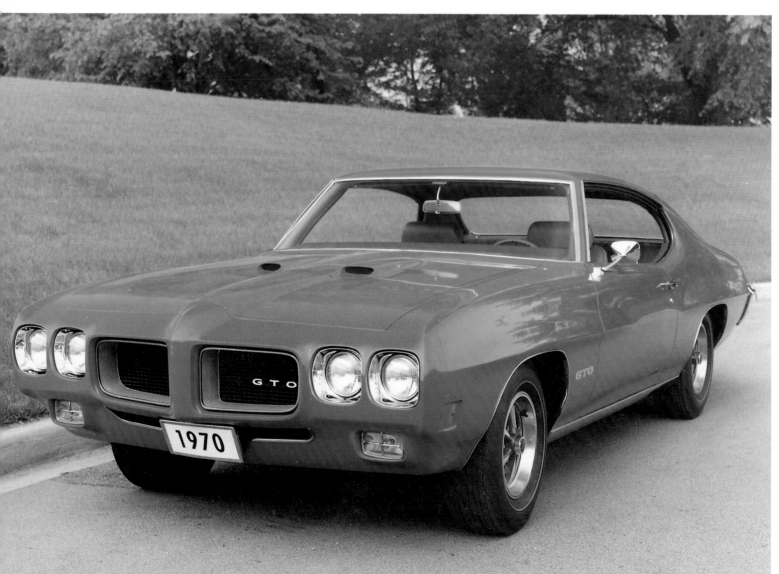

Less outrageous than the yellow ragtop overleaf, but still eye-catching enough, was this white 1970 GTO Judge hardtop (ABOVE). Judge interiors (LEFT) were restrained compared to the rest of the car, but there was that unmistakeable logo on the glove box lid.

Altogether more serious – and a lot more expensive and exclusive – was the Firebird Trans Am. The example pictured (RIGHT) has the 400-cubic-inch V8 with Ram Air IV option and 370bhp. Nose styling of the Firebird had been brought into line with that of the GTO in February 1970.

Pontiac's "new" 455 in the GTO came from the big Bonneville, but unlike Buick and Oldsmobile, they didn't stop production of their existing 400-cubic-inch engine, which they still needed for the Firebird. So the 1970 GTO – restyled for this year with a four-lamp bumper/nose in Endura and pronounced "eyebrows" over its wheelarches – came with no fewer than five engine options. The 400s had 350bhp, or 370bhp with Ram Air. Fastest of the lot was the 400 with Ram Air IV, but the hefty torque of the 455s made them more streetable performance motors, and most buyers preferred them.

Young kids could still buy the GTO Judge in 1970, this time tricked out with loud sidestripes over the wheelarch eyebrows and a new style of rear spoiler. Standard motor was the 366bhp Ram Air III version of the 400; the 370bhp Ram Air IV was optional; and the 360bhp 455 became optional toward the end of the season. Once again, the car represented good value for money in the performance market despite its slightly tacky image, but sales followed the year's depressing downward trend.

The sales slump didn't do justice to the excellence of the 1970 Firebird, either, although the car didn't appear until February 1970 and therefore suffered from a curtailed season. This second-generation car had been developed jointly by Pontiac and Chevrolet (who used essentially the same design for their Camaro), and was undoubtedly the best Firebird yet. Longer, lower, and wider in the best traditions of the American car industry, it came only as a strikingly attractive hardtop coupé with an Endura bumper/nose which underlined its family relationship with the GTO. There was a four-model range, beginning with the regular Firebird, going on through the sporty Formula 400 and luxurious Esprit, up to the top-performance Trans Am.

Muscle Car enthusiasts eschewed the regular and Esprit models, but looked with interest at the Formula 400. This came with a pair of aggressive-looking scoops on its fiberglass hood, which were purely decorative with the stock 330bhp 400 V8, but became functional when the optional 345bhp Ram Air 400 was fitted. Performance was good but not startling, even with the Ram Air motor, which offered quarter-miles in the mid 14s at 100mph. By contrast, the regular 400 brought lackluster times of 15 seconds at just 93mph.

For more serious performance, there was, of course, the Firebird Trans Am. For 1970, this had several features not available on other Firebirds: a front air dam and rear spoiler, air extractors in the front fenders and fairings head of the rear wheelarches, and a rear-facing shaker hood scoop. The standard Firebird came with the 345bhp Ram-Air 400 which was optional in the Formula 400, but there was also a 370bhp Ram Air IV motor, which brought more serious performance potential. Not many of these were sold, however.

There is a pleasing lack of ornamentation on this 1970 Boss 429 Mustang (LEFT), the biggest-engined but not actually the quickest of Ford's ponycar offerings that year. The matt black hood scoop was unique to 1970 models.

Huge hood stripes nevertheless added distinction to this Chevrolet Chevelle SS 396 (BELOW LEFT), which had the big-bore 402 motor under its hood and either 350 bhp or, rarely, 375bhp.

Chevrolet – a shrinking range

For 1970, Chevrolet performance models were available in three ranges, down from the four of 1969. The Camaro once again represented the division among ponycar muscle machines, among compacts there was still the Nova, and at the intermediate level the Chevelle still wore the bow tie with pride.

Like Buick, Chevrolet had to develop a new engine to meet the new GM 455-cubic-inch ceiling for their intermediates, but unlike Buick, they were able to draw on existing hardware. They simply took the big-block 427 and gave it a longer stroke, which produced a 454-cubic-inch capacity engine.

The 454 immediately became the top performance engine in the well-proportioned new Chevelle range, which now bore a closer family resemblance to the full-size Chevrolets. In the SS 454, it came in standard LS-5 tune with 360bhp and hydraulic lifters, or in temperamental 450bhp LS-6 dragstrip tune with solid lifters. The 450bhp motor had plenty of torque and gave smart getaways on strip or street, but performance tailed off at higher revs and an SS 454 with the LS-6 wouldn't reach 100mph in the quarter, despite a time of around 13.7 seconds. Farther down the model hierarchy, there was

still the Chevelle SS 396, fitted after January 1970 with the big-bore 402 motor. Power outputs remained unchanged throughout the season, with 350bhp from the base L-34 engine and 375bhp from the rare L-78.

The 396 motor still provided the motive power for the hottest Nova SS, the SS 396. The 1970 Nova was changed from its 1969 incarnation in only cosmetic details, and was just as quick as its predecessor. However, competition in this sector of the market was hotting up, with Plymouth's Duster 340 a particularly strong challenger, and at the end of the season Chevrolet decided to withdraw the Nova. The SS 396 therefore disappeared.

The 1970 Camaros did not appear until February that year, thoroughly redesigned and sporting what many believe to have been the most attractive Camaro styling ever. Hot SS 396 models were still listed, although there were now just two states of tune instead of three: the 325bhp option had gone, leaving only the 350bhp and 375bhp types. The 1970 models had no special trim, although badges did distinguish them from the herd of lesser Camaros, and they could once again be had with a special Rally Sport nose as an option.

This year's Z-28 Camaro might just have been the best of its kind. Sharing its good looks with other Camaro models, it sported a new engine – the LT-1 Corvette 350 V8, slightly detuned to give 360bhp. In street versions, it gave 60mph from rest in under six seconds and was capable of powering the car to quarter-miles in the low 14s at just over 100mph. Handling was also excellent, but the Z-28s failed to win the Trans Am series in 1970, where they had to concede victory to the Boss 302 Mustangs.

Ford and Mercury – cutting back

The signs were unmistakeable during 1970: Ford did not intend to remain in the Muscle Car business for much longer. There had been another management shake-up, when Lee Iacocca had taken over from Bunkie Knudsen as Chairman, and among the first things he did was to kill off the Shelby Mustangs.

There *were* some 1970 Shelby Mustangs, both GT-350s and GT-500s, but they were simply leftover 1969 models, updated with an extra spoiler and a few other items. Once they had gone, Ford muscle fans had to settle for the Mach 1 Mustang. Not that the Mach 1 Mustang was a bad car to settle for. All the 1970 models had the attractive SportsRoof body, complete with the spoilers and side stripes which advertised the model's performance image. Standard once again was the 250bhp 351 Cleveland V8, but a more interesting 300bhp version was optional. Better still was a Cobra Jet with 335bhp and a Ram-Air option, and right at the top was the 375bhp 429. These were tempting packages, but they were not tempting enough to exempt the Mach 1 from the general Mustang sales slide – sales were 43 percent down over 1969.

The Boss Mustangs remained in production for 1970, the Boss 429 being mechanically identical to the 1969 cars and the Boss 302 being changed rather more. Boss 302s driven by Parnelli Jones and George Follmer triumphed in

the Trans Am series this year, but the new Iacocca regime reasoned that even this would not justify keeping the model in the Mustang line-up for 1971.

Most important of the 1970 changes for the Boss 302 were to the engine, where smaller valves and other modifications had been forced upon Ford by emissions control regulations. Street versions still claimed 290bhp, which was still an under-estimate, but there wasn't much doubt that power was down. New front and rear styling details and hockey-stick side stripes kept the visual appeal alive, and distinguished the Boss 302 at a glance from its bigger-engined Boss 429 relative. In appearance at least, this was still a much more subtle piece of performance machinery than either the Boss 429 or the Mach 1 cars; but it was also expensive, and quarter-miles at around 103mph in a shade over 14 seconds weren't enough to tempt more than about 500 buyers this year.

Among the intermediates, Ford's 1970 muscle model was the Cobra, a fastback coupé on the Torino line. Last season's budget-muscle Cobra 428 now had the 360bhp 429 V8 as standard, but it had also put on weight. Six-second 0 to 60mph sprints were good news on the street,

The 1970 Mustang was undoubtedly one of the most attractive versions of Ford's ponycar, and the subtle side-striping which distinguished the hot Boss 302 version betrayed more taste than some other manufacturers seemed to have at the time. Advertised horsepower remained at 290, but the 1970 engine had smaller valves than its 1969 counterpart to meet exhaust emissions regulations and improve driveability. In street trim, the 1970 Boss 302 would hit 60mph in well under seven seconds and ran quarter-miles in the high 14s. Competition versions ran away with that year's Trans Am championship.

The big fastbacks from Ford and Mercury scored on looks if not on outright performance during 1970. Left is the Mercury Cyclone 429, and below the GT version of the same car. On the right, the red car is Ford's Torino GT with the 429 Super Cobra Jet motor, and at bottom right its big-block V8 shows off the shaker hood scoop which was then fashionable among performance car fans.

but quarters in the mid-14s kept this Torino derivative out of the front ranks of Muscle Cars for 1970.

Meanwhile, Mercury's muscle offerings came in the same two Cougar and Cyclone ranges as last year. The Cougar had been updated only cosmetically, with a split grille and other detail changes, but the Cyclone had increased in size along with the rest of the Montego range from which it was derived, and now sat on a 117-inch wheelbase. Its distinguishing feature was an ugly central "nose" on the grille, and the Spoiler derivative's front air dam, rear aerofoil, huge air scoop, and hood-mounted tachometer did nothing to improve the looks.

Cyclones came with 351 or 390 V8s as before, or with the 429 V8 motor in place of last year's 428. The basic tune for this motor was 360bhp, but the Spoiler edition came with 370bhp and there was an optional 375bhp Super Cobra Jet motor with Ram Air. It all sounded exciting, but like so many other muscle machines in 1970, the Cyclones failed to sell in large numbers.

To give the Cougar Eliminator a more memorable street-performance image for 1970, Mercury offered it with three performance packages, which went by the names of Impressor, Controller, and Dominator. The 351 Windsor and the 390 weren't offered this year; instead the Eliminator had Ford's new 351 Cleveland V8, offering

Mercury's Cougar ragtop (ABOVE LEFT) was more for show than for go in 1970, with just 250bhp from its 351-cubic-inch V8. However, the yellow hardtop Cougar Eliminator pictured (LEFT) offered much better performance from its 290bhp 302 Boss Mustang engine – and the decals did wonders for its image.

AMC's unique AMX coupé (ABOVE) was still quick, but failed to attract big sales.

300bhp. There was a Ram Air option, too. Alternative motors were the 428 Super Cobra Jet with 335bhp, the Boss 429 with 375bhp, and the Boss 302, this year with bottom-end torque to give the Eliminator smarter step-offs. But it was all largely to no avail. The 1970 Cougar Eliminator was too heavy to keep up with the pack.

AMC

AMC couldn't field the Scrambler again for 1970, because the model on which it was based had ceased production. Instead, they put forward The Machine, a much larger car based on their 114-inch wheelbase Rebel intermediate. The AMX, now in its third year, picked up some welcome improvements, but still didn't sell well enough for AMC to persuade its makers to keep it alive for 1971.

The AMX followed the Javelin from which it was derived in most details of its 1970 facelift. Most obvious were a restyled front end with a new grille, and a hood equipped with a center scoop. When the Ram Air 340 V8

The AMC AMX 390 was in its last year during 1970 (LEFT). It shared its 390 V8 with the Rebel Machine (RIGHT) – more show than go but still a desirable Muscle Car. The 390 motor is shown in the sedan (BELOW RIGHT).

Muscle Car Choice – 1970

Subcompacts
AMC AMX 390

Compacts
Chevrolet Nova SS 396
Plymouth Duster 340

Ponycars
Chevrolet Camaro SS 396
Chevrolet Camaro Z-28
Dodge Challenger R/T
Dodge Challenger T/A
Ford Mustang Boss 302
Ford Mustang Boss 429
Ford Mustang Mach 1
(with 428 or 429 option)
Mercury Cougar
Eliminator
Plymouth AAR 'Cuda
Plymouth 'Cuda
Pontiac Firebird Formula
400 (with Ram-Air option)
Pontiac Firebird Trans Am
Shelby Mustang GT-350
Shelby Mustang GT-500

Intermediates
AMC Rebel Machine
Buick GSX
Chevrolet Chevelle SS 396
Chevrolet Malibu SS 454
Dodge Coronet R/T
Ford Cobra 428
Mercury Cyclone Spoiler
Oldsmobile 4-4-2
Plymouth GTX
Plymouth Road Runner
Superbird
Pontiac GTO
Pontiac GTO Judge

was fitted, this scoop came with vacuum-operated flaps. Otherwise, the engine bay contained the good old 390 V8, this year with a lower compression to meet emissions control demands but up by 10bhp to 325bhp. A good AMX coupé could still reach 60mph in 6.6 seconds, with quarter-mile times in the mid-14s at 92mph.

Much the same performance could be had from the Rebel Machine, which had the same 390 V8. It should have been faster, but suffered from severe wheel hop under fierce acceleration and therefore had problems on both street and strip. But AMC hadn't lost their knack of making a car look good. The first 1000 Rebel Machines came in the familiar red, white, and blue colors, and all 2326 had a hood scoop with vacuum-operated air vents and a tacho embedded in the driver's side. Heavy-duty suspension gave the car a nose-down look and dual exhausts completed the picture. There were several dealer performance options, but the Rebel Machine was ultimately an also-ran in the history of the Muscle Car.

1971

On the Slope

If there ever was a bad year for Muscle Car fans, it was 1971. The writing had been on the wall for some time, but in 1971 the Muscle Car market collapsed completely, dipping even lower than the depressing 1970 season. In that year, low sales of high-performance cars could perhaps have been shrugged off in the light of low overall sales for new cars. In 1971, however, new car sales bounced back to a record high, exceeding the 1970 total by some 16 percent. Against this background, the continued decline of Muscle Car sales stood out in very stark contrast.

There were several reasons for this collapse. Higher insurance premiums for big-block Muscle Cars had been threatening sales for some time and had now had a devastating effect: the youngsters to whom the factory-built hot rods most appealed could no longer afford to run them. Public opinion was also turning against high-performance cars in an era when safety was increasingly becoming the motorist's primary preoccupation, and high performance was seen as the antithesis of safety. Then there were increases in purchase cost caused by the increases in manufacturing costs which in turn were brought about by the additional safety and emissions control equipment which new cars had to carry. The extra equipment added weight, and Detroit was no longer able to offset this weight by boosting power and torque because the tighter emissions control regulations were gradually strangling engine outputs.

Before long, all new cars sold in the U.S.A. would have to run on lead-free gasoline, and during 1971 many automakers introduced their first engines tuned to run on lead-free fuel. Compression ratios had to come down to suit this low-octane gasoline, and power figures tumbled. Some makers held out during 1971, retaining high compression engines as far as they could for their high-performance cars, but others anticipated the new regulations and brought to market engines which had been detuned for lead-free fuel and had lost power by the truckload. When General Motors instructed its divisions to lower their engine's compression ratios across the board for the 1971 models, the result was power losses of as much as 12 percent.

Chrysler's Dodge and Plymouth divisions, which had

Muscle Cars still looked good for 1971, but they were a dying breed and didn't have the performance of their predecessors. On the left is a '71 Dodge Charger; on the right a Plymouth Road Runner. Over the page, the Road Runner shows off its garish paint job and side stripes.

been in the forefront of the Muscle Car market for so long, retained high compressions for 1971. However, they took to publishing two sets of horsepower figures: one was the usual gross rating, and the other was the SAE net rating, which was the engine's output with all ancillaries like the clutch, the alternator, and power steering attached, which was much lower than the gross figure. Next year, the net figures would be the only figures used by the whole industry.

The major automakers also declined to take part in the SCCA's Trans Am series for 1971, with the result that the homologation specials were no longer needed and were therefore deleted from the catalogs. For 1971, there were no Boss 302 Mustangs and no AAR 'Cudas, although Pontiac continued to use the Trans Am name to distinguish the hottest of its Firebird models and Chevrolet fielded a lukewarm Z-28 Camaro. At NASCAR, meanwhile, new regulations outlawed Ford's Torino Talladega, Mercury's Cyclone Spoiler II, and the Dodge Charger Daytona and Plymouth Road Runner Superbird. Those in the market for roadgoing high-performance cars were consequently offered fewer models to choose from.

A few brave makers still believed in compact muscle cars as the way forward, but the genre was not an unqualified success. Encouraged by sales of their Dart Swinger 340, Dodge put forward the new Demon 340 which was based on Plymouth's existing Duster 340, and did rather well. AMC's contender, the Hornet SC/360, was nevertheless rewarded with only limited sales. Chevrolet were hanging on in there with the Nova SS, now with smaller V8s than before, but here too sales were disappointing.

Dodge and Plymouth – still hot for '71

On the face of it, Chrysler's MOPAR divisions still believed in high performance for 1971. The mighty Hemi was still available in the intermediates and ponycars for those who wanted blistering performance; the Six-Pack edition of the 440 V8 was only very slightly less powerful than last year; and the up-and-coming muscle compacts with their 340 V8s earned a great deal of respect. In fact, they did very much better than old-style muscle machinery like the Road Runner, which this year was made available with its first small-block motor in order to keep sales alive. However, the new NASCAR rules had succeeded in burying winged wonders like the Charger Daytona and Road Runner Superbird. Not that any of that stopped Plymouth from shining on the superspeedways: they won at NASCAR in 1971 with a total of 22 victories, 21 of them by Richard Petty.

For 1971, Dodge division reorganized its intermediate ranges around two new wheelbase lengths. Two-doors sat on 115-inch wheelbases and four-doors used 117-inch wheelbases; Coronets were all four-doors this year, and so the budget-muscle Super Bee moved over to the two-door Charger line.

The Chargers were in fact the largest of Dodge's muscle machines this year, but were two inches shorter in the wheelbase than last season's Chargers. As part of the model range realignment, they had been completely restyled and now boasted a svelte new "coke-bottle" shape with a semi-fastback roofline. Base-model Chargers held no interest for hard-core muscle enthusiasts, but the Charger R/T and Charger Super Bee were still serious performance machinery.

Dodge had made sure they looked the part, too. The R/T was distinguished from its stablemates by non-functional hood vents, simulated air scoops in the doors, and racing stripes on the hood and sides. Spoilers for front and rear could be specified on the order form, and added to the visual impact if not to the road-holding at speeds lower than those needed on the NASCAR ovals. Super Bee models looked plainer, but were still very obviously performance-oriented.

Engine options in the Super Bee started with the 383 V8, which offered 275bhp or 300bhp, and even in the higher state of tune this was 35bhp down on 1970's offering in the superseded Coronet Super Bee. The R/T could

The 1971 Dodge Super Bee was a Charger derivative; earlier models had been based on the Coronet. This example, with typically loud paint job, has the optional 440 Magnum V8 with 370bhp – not a bad figure, although it was down on last year's. The hood scoop added to the aggressive appearance.

be had with the 440 Magnum in 370bhp or 385bhp 440-6 tune, both versions just 5bhp down on last year's figures. Lastly, both R/T and Super Bee were available with the Hemi, although no more than 100 Chargers of all types came with this 425bhp option. Hemi Chargers had a vacuum operated hood scoop instead of the decorative louvers fitted to other performance Chargers.

The Hemi-powered Chargers were still a force to be reckoned with, not least at NASCAR where they performed well during 1971. On the street, they would reach 60mph in under six seconds, and at the strips they turned quarter-miles in 13.7 seconds at 104mph. The 440-6 was ultimately more manageable on the street, however, and the Hemi remained largely the preserve of those who wanted a Charger for serious competition use.

The Challenger, Dodge's 110-inch-wheelbase ponycar, was largely carried over from 1970. It picked up a new grille but very little else which suggested that Dodge wanted to improve its appeal. In fact, the Challenger range was considerably realigned for 1971. A T/A model

was advertised but never made (Dodge didn't need it because they were no longer involved in Trans Am racing), the R/T convertible was dropped, and the SE package was available only on base-model Challengers.

The R/T for '71 had color-keyed bumpers, dummy brake cooling slots on its rear flanks, and new tape stripes. The standard motor in those Challengers with performance pretensions was the 383 V8, now down to 300bhp because of its lowered compression, and the base 440 Magnum wasn't available any longer. Buyers could order the 440-6 with 385bhp – again down on 1970's figures – and a few Hemi Challengers were also made. Challenger sales were not good, though. In 1971, only the second year for Dodge's ponycar, sales of the range dropped by almost 60 percent. Sales of the performance derivatives suffered accordingly.

A small group of Dodge dealers attempted to boost Challenger sales during 1971 by providing 50 specially-prepared examples as official and pace cars for the Indianapolis 500 race. All these cars were convertibles

finished in Hemi Orange with white seats, although just two of them had high-performance options fitted. One – the pace car – skidded when leaving the track after the warm-up lap and crashed into a press box, injuring a number of reporters. Not surprisingly, the decal sets available through Dodge dealers to make pace-car replicas during 1971 didn't sell in large numbers after that.

Smallest of the 1971 hot Dodges was the Demon, which had the same 108-inch fastback body as Plymouth's Duster compact. Grille and tail details differentiated the two. Top performance option was the Demon 340, which replaced the Dart Swinger 340 in Dodge's line-up and was a sight more interesting than the lukewarm slant-six and 318 V8 Demons which fitted in further down the range. The Demon 340 came with Dodge's well-liked 275bhp 340 small-block V8, still with the high compression ratio it had boasted in 1970, and the car could be tricked out with a twin-scoop hood, spoilers, Rallye wheels, and all the other goodies it needed to give it the right visual appeal.

Much the same could be said for the Demon's Plymouth Duster 340 sister, which sold to the tune of 13,000 examples during 1971. Plymouth division followed a different policy from Dodge, lowering the 340 V8's compression but making up the deficiency with a new carburetor so that they could still list the motor at 275bhp. Visually, the Duster 340 was changed from the 1970 edition by large "340" decals on the rear fenders, by a new grille and rear lamps, and by the optional matt-black hood with a huge "340" decal offset to the driver's side. But it wasn't news for 1971. For that, Plymouth fans had to look farther down the performance scale to the Duster Twister, which was essentially an appearance package allied to a lower-powered Duster; or to the new Scamp, which was Plymouth's answer to the Dodge Dart Swinger. Plymouth had calculated – correctly – that more decals would earn them better sales in '71 than more horsepower.

Next up in size at Plymouth was the Barracuda, which was essentially the same as the new model introduced for

Smallest of the MoPar Muscle Cars for 1971 were the Dodge Demon and Plymouth Duster, both on 108-inch wheelbases and both equipped with the 340 V8 in 275bhp tune – although there were differences between the engines. On the right, the Plymouth version of the engine sits in a '71 Duster, while the Duster 340 (ABOVE) shows off its typically eye-catching purple paint job. The appearance of the Dodge Demon 340 (ABOVE LEFT) is positively restrained in comparison!

1970 but had a segmented grille with twin headlamps, dummy front fender vents, and segmented tail lamps. There were six-cylinder engines and a 318-cubic-inch V8 at the bottom of the range, but the 383 could also be had in two states of tune. Performance-oriented Barracudas once again went under the name of 'Cuda, and started with the 340 V8, going on up through a four-barrel 383 with 300bhp and a 440 Six-Pack with 385bhp to the all-out 425bhp Hemi. Just 115 Hemi 'Cudas were sold, and even a new and garish tape stripe option couldn't give the 'Cuda enough appeal to prevent the same sales slide seen almost everywhere else in the Muscle Car market.

Plymouth's hot intermediates for 1971 were slightly smaller than 1970's, with wheelbases an inch shorter at 115 inches. Their new styling was curvaceous and very attractive, and all came with wider rear tracks to improve handling. Just as over at Dodge, the division had restructured its range around two wheelbases, and four-door sedans and wagons had 117-inch wheelbases while all the two-doors rode the 115-inch platform. The performance Road Runner and GTX models both used the hardtop coupé body, and could be had with a variety of engine options.

The Road Runner was still very much a budget intermediate muscle machine, but it was not the performance car it had been. At the beginning of the year, the standard

Muscle versions of the Plymouth Barracuda were all badged as 'Cudas for 1971. Above is an entry-level 383 model, and on the left is its powerplant. On the right is the 440 Six-Pack and above it a Hemi 'Cuda in Plymouth's unforgettable purple.

More hot Plymouths from '71: above is a Hemi-powered Road Runner,
while the main picture shows the more common 440-engined model.
Above right, is a GTX, also equipped with the 440 Super Commando V8.

engine was still the 383 V8, although now putting out just 300bhp instead of last year's 335bhp. In the heavier shell, it inevitably made for a slower car. The Road Runner 440+6 came with 385bhp and the triple-two-barrel carburetor package; and of course there was the Hemi with 425bhp, but that attracted just 55 buyers during 1971. Most of the '71 options for the Road Runner contributed more to appearance than to performance, although the Air Grabber hood managed to improve both aspects to some extent.

Sales were sliding, though. To buck things up, Plymouth introduced a low-priced Road Runner with the 340 V8 at mid-season, which might have attracted a few buyers but wasn't what the Road Runner had always been about. Even with the regular 300bhp 383, a 1971 Road Runner needed nearly 15 seconds to run the quarter-mile, and its trap speed of less than 95mph was none too impressive; the six-barrel 440 couldn't improve on those figures, either, and street acceleration of 6.7 seconds for the 0 to 60mph sprint made clear that the Road Runner was a spent force. Sales figures backed that up. What had once been Plymouth's best-selling hot intermediate bottomed out at just over 14,000 in 1971 as compared to some 43,500 in 1970.

The GTX fared badly, too, selling fewer than 3000 units this year as against nearer 8000 in 1970. Not surprisingly,

1971 turned out to be the model's last appearance. As was the case with so many other hot machines at this time, what killed it was a combination of increased weight with decreased power. In fact, power wasn't down all that seriously for 1971: the 440 Super Commando V8 in four-barrel form was down by just 5bhp to 370bhp, and the 440-6 and Hemi options were unchanged with 390bhp and 425bhp respectively. Quarter-miles of very nearly 15 seconds at 95mph with the standard motor were just average, however.

The 1971 Mach 1 Mustang from Ford had the new SportsRoof body, and there wasn't much doubt by this stage that Ford knew how to make a car look good – both inside and out – even if performance was on the wane. This car, however, is fitted with the higher-powered version of the 351 Cleveland V8 motor, which made it fast by 1971 standards.

Ford and Mercury – getting fatter

Ford didn't put up a budget to back racers in NASCAR or the SCCA Trans Am series in 1971, and as a result only three NASCAR races went to Ford-badged cars. This was the maker's worst season at the superspeedways since 1955. The effects of Ford's withdrawal from competition were also immediately obvious on the performance cars available through the showrooms. This year's Mustangs were the biggest and heaviest there had ever been, and they lacked either a Boss 302 or a Boss 429 variant. The only Boss Mustang available had the 351 Cleveland V8, which made it quite a performer although the car didn't have the charisma of its predecessors. In the intermediate line, there were still hot fastbacks, but the Cobra sold at about half the level of 1970 sales.

The 1971 Cobra was carried over from 1970, freshened slightly with some minor cosmetic touches. Standard equipment was the 351 Cleveland V8 in four-barrel form, with 285bhp as against last season's 300bhp. The 429 was still available, either with or without Ram Air, and the same 370bhp was claimed for both versions. This, at least, was only 5bhp down on 1970's figures, but it didn't make the Cobra a winner.

There was just one advantage of the wider new body on 1971 Mustangs: it allowed enough room around the big-block 429 for enthusiasts to work on Ford's hottest motor, which last year had been a very tight fit under the Mustang's hood. It wasn't available in the lower-order Mustangs, of course, though it was one of several options in the Mach 1 performance range.

All the Mach 1 Mustangs for 1971 had the new Sports-Roof body, with its almost flat roofline. Most had the optional twin-scoop hood, which was functional only when Ram Air was specified, and all of them had the Competition Suspension set-up which made them handle pretty well. The standard model had the 351 Cleveland in 285bhp tune, but a 330bhp option was also available. Top of the performance options were two versions of the 429 engine: a new 370bhp four-barrel Cobra Jet motor, and the 375bhp Super Cobra Jet with Ram Air induction. "Drag Pack" editions of both engines, with solid lifters and a high-lift camshaft, were rated at 375bhp. However, these big-block Mustangs didn't handle as well as their smaller-engined brethren and the poor sales figures reflected the doubts many potential buyers must have had after trying one out.

The performance spotlight in any case fell on the Boss 351 Mustang, which replaced the Boss 302 homologation special that Ford no longer needed now they weren't involved in Trans Am racing. Like the Mach 1, it had the SportsRoof body with a twin-scoop hood. It also had the Competition Suspension package but with additional tweaks and fatter tires which made it handle even better than the Mach 1. The only engine option was the High Output 351 Cleveland V8 with Ram Air and 330bhp, and that made it a first-division performer on the street. Zero to 60mph could be polished off in 5.8 seconds, which was very much up with the front-runners for 1971. At the strips, though, the Boss 351 wasn't quite so spectacular. Quarters took just over 14 seconds with a trap speed of a fraction over 100mph.

Only one version of the 429, a 370bhp Super Cobra Jet with Ram Air, turned up in Mercury products for 1971. Mercury, in fact, was determined to get out of performance cars and back into its traditional luxury lines as soon as it possibly could. Those NASCAR entrants who depended on the make were none too impressed with the factory's latest offerings, and turned instead to 1969-model Cyclones. Ironically, these older models achieved the Mercury badge's best-ever NASCAR season in 1971, with 11 wins.

The 1971 Cyclones came with the 351 Cleveland as standard, with a paltry 240bhp in the mid-range GT model and 285bhp in the regular hardtop. The Ram Air 429 was standard on the Spoiler and optional on the other two Cyclone models. A GT was quick on the street, needing 6.4 seconds to reach 60mph from rest when the stoplights turned green, but it needed 14.5 seconds at the strip to run the quarter-mile.

Buick, Oldsmobile, and Pontiac – down on power, down on sales

GM's Buick, Oldsmobile, and Pontiac divisions fielded the same line-up of Muscle Cars for 1971 as they had for 1970. From Buick came the GS and GSX, from Oldsmobile came the 4-4-2, and from Pontiac came the GTO, GTO Judge, Firebird, and Firebird Trans Am. However, lowered compression ratios in all models took power away and the 1971 ranges could not equal the performance figures of earlier times. The market demanded appearance and comfort options, and GM responded appropriately, but sales still declined.

At Oldsmobile, the 4-4-2 sold just 7500 units this year, which compared badly with the 1970 total of well over 19,000. The slow-selling Sports Coupé model had gone, leaving only the convertible and Holiday coupé in production. The four-barrel 455 V8 was still standard, but power was now down to 340bhp from last year's 365bhp, and the W-30 top performance option had just 350bhp instead of last year's 370bhp. When quoted in the SAE net figures which would become the industry standard during 1972, those 350bhp dropped to 300bhp, which made the car appear very much less attractive on paper.

Power was down in the Buick performance cars, too. The entry-level GS 350 (never a serious Muscle Car) was down from 315bhp to 260bhp; the GS 455 had 315bhp instead of 350bhp; and the Stage I motor with Cool-Air induction was down from 360bhp to 345bhp. The lowest of the axle ratio options disappeared for 1971, as Buick veered away from dragstrip stormers. Even so, the right options on a Stage I GS 455 made the car capable of 14-second quarters at 103mph, which put it among the front runners for 1971. This year's GSX still had high-profile

The Boss 351 Mustang had the 330bhp Ram Air motor (RIGHT) and suspension modifications, which made it the best-handling of 1971's Mustangs. With the right choice of paint colors, it looked a million dollars (BELOW). Ford's Torino GT retained its attractive appearance (BELOW LEFT), but performance wasn't great. These would be the last unit-construction Torinos; the all-new 1972 models would revert to body-on-frame construction,

Buyers lost interest in the Oldsmobile 4-4-2 (LEFT AND BELOW), and the end-of-season sales figures were abysmal. The W-30 performance package (BELOW RIGHT) had more to offer than the regular model, but not enough to keep interest alive.

Buick's GSX (RIGHT) was also a sales disaster. It wasn't as if these were bad cars, either – the Muscle Car market had simply died around them.

graphics, but these could also be had at extra cost on other GS models. Sales figures were disastrous, however: only just over 9000 of this year's two models were sold, compared with more than 20,000 of the three models offered by Buick in 1970.

Pontiac were unable to boast greater success. This year's GTOs were incorporated into the Le Mans range, and just over 10,500 of all types were shipped; last year there had been more than 40,000. Revised sheet metal with a rather ugly "snout" grille and hood scoops which had moved forward to give a more streamlined appearance might not have helped sales very much, but the biggest problem must have been the GTO's loss of power. The Ram Air III and Ram Air IV high-performance options were no longer listed, and the standard motor was now a 300bhp edition of the 400, down from last year's 350bhp. A High Output 455 was optional, but it mustered just 335bhp with the standard three-speed or optional four-speed manual transmissions, and was detuned to 325bhp when automatic transmission was supplied.

The GTO Judge had clearly had its day. It shared the sheet metal and front end revisions of the regular GTO, but still wore last year's graphics. The only engine option was the High Output 455 with 335bhp. Sales were so bad that the model was discontinued at mid-year after just 357 hardtops and 17 convertibles had been shipped; last year there had been 3629 hardtops and 168 convertibles.

The focus of high-performance motoring at Pontiac was in any case shifting away from the intermediate GTO and toward the Firebird ponycar. This year, the Firebird Trans Am picked up the 455 motor, adding sparkle to a

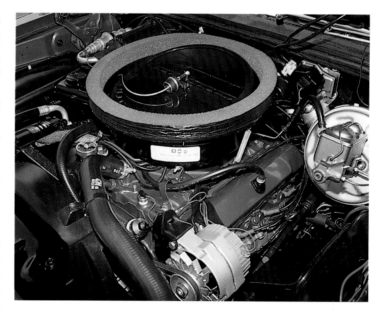

range which was otherwise losing power and performance. Best of the rest was the Formula, this year down to a 250bhp 350 V8 as standard, but still available with the 400-cubic-inch V8; power was down, of course, to 300bhp from 330bhp. However, even the Trans Am's 455 with 325bhp or 335bhp in High Output form didn't have the all-out performance of the previous year's 366bhp Ram Air 400 option.

In one way, though, the 455 in the Trans Am was an improvement. Despite its lowered compression, it had been tuned for bottom-end torque, with the result that the car was more streetable than it had been. Unfortunately that didn't help sales. Firebird Trans Am sales were around one-third down in 1971 at just over 2100 copies.

Chevrolet

For 1971, performance models took a low priority at Chevrolet. There *were* hot Novas, Camaros, and Chevelles, but not many buyers seem to have cared. Chevrolet themselves didn't seem too interested, either. The 111-inch Nova couldn't be bought with the 396 performance V8 any more, and the best motor on offer to performance fans in this model was a 270bhp four-barrel 350 V8. Last year, that same engine had boasted 300bhp; this year, the Nova wasn't a real performance car at all.

The 396 hadn't died altogether, of course: it was still available in the Chevelle SS, now displacing 402 cubic inches and confusingly named the Turbo-Jet 400. Its 300bhp sounded quite impressive until compared with last year's 350bhp in regular trim and 375bhp in L-78 tune. Right at the top of the range, the top-option SS 454 with the LS-6 motor had disappeared, too, although the basic LS-5 version now had 365bhp – five horses more than last year in spite of its lower compression ratio! New cylinder heads and a new camshaft helped to keep power up here, and the 1971 the Chevelle SS 454 was still a muscular little coupé.

The Camaros had lost it, however. Top option was the 330bhp Z-28, with its 350-cubic-inch motor down on power from last year's 360bhp. Next came the 300bhp Turbo-Jet 400, and below that Camaro power outputs didn't fall into the high performance category. The '71 Camaros were pretty enough, but they weren't serious Muscle Cars any more.

AMC – still trying

With the AMX and the Rebel Machine no longer listed for 1971 as a result of 1970's poor sales, AMC turned to a pair of new performance models. In place of the AMX came a Javelin derivative called the AMX 401, and in place of the Rebel Machine came a compact muscle sedan based on the Hornet range. AMC called it the Hornet SC/360.

Hornets had been introduced for 1970 and had 108-inch wheelbases. Entry-level models had six-cylinder power, but AMC made 304 and 360 V8s optional on the '71s to give the range more performance appeal. They created the SC/360 out of a two-door base-model sedan, decked out with appropriate striping and equipped with the larger of the two V8s. This came in 245bhp two-barrel form or as a 285bhp four-barrel with Ram Air in the optional "Go" package. Heavy-duty suspension was standard, and a Twin-Grip limited-slip differential was optional. In 185bhp form, the SC/360 would turn quarter-miles in just under 15 seconds at a little over 95mph, which was reasonable for this year of emasculated Muscle Cars but wasn't anything for performance fans to get excited about. And indeed, they didn't get too excited: AMC couldn't shift more than 784 of their hot compacts this season, and didn't bother to field the SC/360 again in the following season.

The Javelin was new for 1971, and now rode on a longer 110-inch wheelbase. Following current ponycar trends, it was longer, wider, lower – and heavier, which probably explains why AMC thought it necessary to develop a more powerful V8 for the top performance option. Standard in the Javelin AMX was the 245bhp 360; next up was the 285bhp four-barrel; and right at the top stood the 330bhp 401, which was a bored and stroked version of AMC's other V8s and could also be had in the 122-inch wheelbase Ambassador flagship model.

All versions of the Javelin AMX came with the front and rear spoilers that were optional on lesser Javelins; all had their own distinctive grille; and many were equipped with the optional cowl-induction hood. The optional "Go" package was mainly for appearance, however, adding only a Twin-Grip differential and a heavy-duty cooling system to the performance package; hood stripes, slotted steel wheels from last year's Rebel Machine, and a special instrument pack completed the picture. Around 745 Javelin AMX models had the 401 option, and offered their owners quarter-miles in the mid-14s at 93mph. Next year's 401 would be so heavily detuned, however, that it no longer qualified as real muscle machinery.

Pontiac's GTO (LEFT) didn't sell well during 1971, but the reason wasn't only that ugly nose job.

The Firebird Trans Am looked just as good as it always had (ABOVE RIGHT AND OVERLEAF), but sales nose-dived along with those of Muscle Cars in general.

AMC's Hornet SC/360 (RIGHT) was something of a last-ditch attempt, but it was unable to carve itself a real niche in the market and was dropped for 1972.

Muscle Car Choice – 1971

Compacts
AMC Hornet SC/360
Chevrolet Nova SS 396
Dodge Demon 340
Plymouth Duster 340

Ponycars
AMC Javelin AMX 401
Dodge Challenger R/T
Ford Mustang Boss 351
Ford Mustang Mach 1
(with 429 option)
Plymouth 'Cuda (with 383, 440, or Hemi option)
Pontiac Firebird Formula 400
Pontiac Firebird Trans Am

Intermediates
Buick GSX
Chevrolet Malibu SS 454
Dodge Charger R/T
Dodge Charger Super Bee
Ford Cobra 429
Mercury Cyclone Spoiler
Oldsmobile 4-4-2
Plymouth GTX
Plymouth Road Runner
(with 383, 440, or Hemi option)
Pontiac GTO
Pontiac GTO Judge

1972

Going, Going. . . .

It's not hard to pick out the cars which offered real performance excitement for 1972 because there were so few of them. Big names from the past lingered on – GTO, Road Runner, 4-4-2 and the like – but performance fans had to hunt pretty hard to find something really fast, and then they had to pay serious money for it. A Pontiac Firebird Trans Am was still a fast car, but performance was dropping all round. This year, it wasn't a disgrace for manufacturers to claim quarter-miles in the mid-to-high 15s for their muscle models.

The disastrous 1971 season had ensured that 1972 saw a very much reduced number of muscle models on sale, and the increasing severity of emissions control regulations saw to it that the performance potential of those which were offered for sale was very much reduced. The losses in engine output were masked to a large extent by the industry's wholesale switch to quoting power and torque figures in SAE net (installed, with ancillaries) rather than gross (on the bench) figures. Salesmen dealing with customers who were horrified to find that a 1972 big-block V8 was now quoted at well under 200bhp could argue that the change from last year's figures was purely caused by the new rating method. However, it wasn't that difficult to work out the true losses. Engine ancillaries tended to consume around 50-60bhp (or sometimes more), and adding a figure of this order to the quoted net figure would give a rough idea of the gross figures, which could then be compared with last year's.

The year 1972 actually saw a slight increase in new-car sales as compared to 1971, but that didn't mean the customers were happy with what they were getting. The fact was that adding emissions control equipment to existing engines often didn't produce a very refined powerplant: buyers complained of rough running, poor starting, running-on, increased fuel consumption, and, above all, of poor performance. Not until a new generation of engines arrived, designed to meet exhaust emissions regulations, would these criticisms be silenced.

The 1972 descendants of the Muscle Cars still wore racing stripes and had heavy-duty suspensions with fat tires. By such means, Detroit attempted to reassure the dwindling number of high-performance car buyers that all was still well in their world. But it wasn't, and worse was yet to come.

The 1972 Dodge Challenger (ABOVE RIGHT) still looked the part, and the engine (RIGHT) was still dressed up in traditional Muscle Car fashion. But the big-block V8s had gone. That impressive-looking lump under the hood was nothing more than a 340 with just 240bhp.

The Dodge Charger (LEFT AND OVERLEAF) was still listed with the 440 Magnum, however, this version only has the 340 Magnum under its hood.

Dodge and Plymouth

The worst news for hard-core muscle fans must have been that the legendary Hemi had ceased to be a line-production option for 1972. At least that saved it from the indignity of being advertised with net brake horsepower figures (which would probably have been around 370-375bhp). And for competition only, it could still be ordered over the parts counters.

However, the loss of the Hemi took the top street power option away from Dodge and Plymouth at a stroke. The 440 six-barrel – always a close contender for the Hemi, at least on the street – could still be had, but its availability was more restricted than before. It still demanded premium gasoline, but this year it was rated at 330bhp net, down from last year's 385bhp gross. Four-barrel 440s were also available in a limited number of cars and, like the six-barrel versions, they demanded premium fuel. They now offered 280bhp as compared to the 370bhp in 1971 models.

Lower down the scale, it hadn't been possible to make the 383 V8 run satisfactorily on low-lead gasoline, and that engine had disappeared from both Dodge and Plymouth line-ups. In its place came a 400-cubic-inch V8, which was essentially a big-bore 383. This one offered 255bhp net. Finally, the success of the 340 V8 in the compact Muscle Cars of the early 1970s had led MoPar to promote it as a performance engine. For 1972, therefore, the 240bhp small-block motor was also fitted to a number of Dodge and Plymouth intermediates and ponycars.

This year, Dodge once again fielded muscle machinery in three market sectors, covering the compact sector with the Demon, the ponycar sector with the Challenger, and the intermediate sector with the Charger. The Demon was very little changed from last year's offering, and even shed a little weight. Its 340 V8 with 240bhp net didn't sound as powerful as last year's edition with 275bhp gross, but this was one area where the buyers weren't complaining. Even so, sales continued to fall.

The 1972 Challenger picked up new frontal styling with an eggcrate grille which had downturned ends. Some said it was pulling a sad face at its own emasculation. The 240bhp 340 motor was the biggest available this year, and there were no convertibles any more. The R/T had also gone, to be replaced by a tepid Rallye edition which mustered no more than 150bhp from its 318-cubic-inch V8. This wasn't a performance car in any sense of the word, even though its appearance might have suggested otherwise.

If the Challenger was a write-off for 1972, fortunately the Charger wasn't. Its range had been dramatically cut, and neither R/T nor Super Bee were now listed, but at least the 440 Magnum V8 was still available, in both four-barrel and Six-Pack versions. There was also a 255bhp 400 V8, which was worth considering. Out on the NAS-CAR tracks, star driver Richard Petty switched from Plymouth to a Dodge Charger in mid-season and won five races with it, clinching the drivers' championship for himself in the process.

Plymouth, too, offered the same three performance-car lines as in 1971 and, like the Dodges, they were not what they had been. Most popular of the lot were the little Duster 340 coupés, which sold 15,681 copies – more than twice as many as the performance-oriented 'Cuda derivative of the Barracuda ponycar. In the intermediate Satellite range, the GTX had disappeared, and only the Road Runner remained of interest to Muscle Car fans.

The Duster 340 was little changed from 1971, although it was now advertised with 240bhp net instead of 275bhp gross. Weight was down; price was up – and so were sales. Overall Barracuda sales were slightly down but, paradoxically, the slimmed-down hot 'Cuda line did better than before. Customers were denied convertible models this year, and the big-block V8s had also disappeared. However, decals and stripes no doubt played their part in improving sales. The matt black "three-runner" hood with body-color sections around its twin scoops certainly made a '72 'Cuda look the part. Sadly, the hottest option was the same 340 V8 which powered the Duster, and a stock 'Cuda this year needed 16 seconds to run the quarter-mile and took 8.5 seconds to hit 60mph on the street.

RIGHT: The Pontiac GTO was definitely past its best by 1972, and certainly wasn't the car it used to be in the 1960s. In fact, this year the GTO ceased to be a model in its own right, becoming merely an option in the Le Mans range.

The Road Runner found just 7628 buyers, which was little more than half last season's total of 14,218. It looked much the same as the 1971 models, although segmented tape stripes running from roof to rear wheelarch were a distinguishing feature. Standard powerplant was the 340 small-block with 240bhp; next up was the new 400 with 255bhp; and a four-barrel 440 topped the range with 280bhp. The Road Runner still had image, but it no longer had real performance.

Ford and Mercury

Ford and Mercury didn't completely abandon big-block V8s for 1972, but the only model in which the 429 Cobra Jet motor could be had this year was the Torino fastback intermediate. Ford Mustangs and Mercury Cougars couldn't go above 351 cubic inches. As for the Cyclone, that had now disappeared completely as Mercury began to concentrate once more on its traditional luxury models.

The Ford Torino was a completely new design this year, and the unit-construction of the superseded model was replaced by body-on-frame construction. Despite a shorter wheelbase of 114 inches instead of 116 inches,

weight therefore went up, which was the last thing the Torino needed at a time when engine power and torque outputs were tumbling. Coil springs replaced the leaf type on the back axle and gave a softer ride, although Ford predictably argued that they also offered handling advantages.

Top Torino was the Gran Torino Sport, which came with the obligatory hood scoop. The Cobra model had gone, but the 429 motor could still be ordered in any Torino – coupé, sedan, and wagon alike. Unfortunately, with just 205bhp in net figures, it was tuned for smooth torque rather than performance, and didn't make the Torino into anybody's street racer. Much more interesting was the four-barrel 351 Cleveland V8, which offered 248bhp and was the most powerful engine in Ford's passenger car line-up that year. Below that, only emasculated V8s and a six were available: the 302 had 140bhp; the two-barrel 351 came with 161bhp; and there was a 400 with 168bhp.

Mustang styling changes were few this year, although there had been serious changes under the hood. All the big-blocks had gone. The Boss 351 had also been dropped, leaving only the Mach 1 as the performance edition.

Standard in this model was the 302 V8, which offered just 140bhp. Better were 177bhp two-barrel and 266bhp four-barrel editions of the 351 V8, but best of the lot was a late introduction designed to boost flagging Mustang sales. This was a 275bhp four-barrel version of the 351, now sporting solid lifters and mated exclusively to a four-speed transmission and a Traction-Lok limited-slip rear end. Only one ratio was available, so Ford clearly weren't about to reverse their policy and start taking this per-formance thing seriously again. And the mid-year Spring decor option (red, white, and blue with a patriotic American flag decal, or a Canadian one for cars sold over the border) was a truer reflection of the way Ford thought their marketing should go.

Mercury racers were still unimpressed by the factory's performance offerings. However, the '69 Torinos which they had raced at NASCAR last season were now too old to qualify under the rules, and so the teams switched to 1971-model Mercury Montegos and carried off nine vic-tories with them in 1972. Performance barely existed in the showroom models, although the Cougar could be had with the 351 V8 in 164bhp, 262bhp, and 266bhp forms, the latter two providing some street interest.

Buick, Oldsmobile, and Pontiac

Performance models from GM's Buick, Pontiac, and Old-smobile divisions were relegated to option status for 1972 as part of a corporate policy to reduce the emphasis on speed. That meant the Buick GS settled back into the Gran Sport range, the Oldsmobile 4-4-2 merged into the

Cutlass series, and the Pontiac GTO was downplayed among the Le Mans models. However, things weren't quite as bad as they appeared on the surface, and those who wanted a hot intermediate still had something worth looking at in GM's showrooms; and for a hot pony-car, it was hard to find anything better than this year's Pontiac Firebird Trans Am.

Buick had dressed the 1972 GS models with minor grille and graphics changes. They had dropped the GSX, but the big-block motors were still on offer. While the entry-level GS engine was the 350 V8, now advertised at just 195bhp, the regular 455 four-barrel promised 250bhp and the Stage I claimed 270bhp. In these hard times, out-puts of this order were not to be sniffed at, although customers for the hottest GS models were few. Toward the end of the season, Buick dealers offered a perform-ance hop-up with Stage II cylinder heads. The Buick was still a performance car this year, taking just 5.8 seconds to reach 60mph and running quarter-miles in a fraction over 14 seconds. Performance fans must have been reassured that someone still cared about them.

Over at Oldsmobile, though, they might have had their doubts. The 4-4-2 option was no longer tied to a specific engine, but instead was listed as an appearance and handling package for the two-door Cutlass and Cutlass S, and for the Cutlass Supreme convertible derivative. It went under the title of option W-29, and consisted of special decals, stripes, and badges, a special grille and lou-vered hood, heavy-duty suspension, and fatter wheels and tires.

Oldsmobile's 4-4-2 (LEFT) was relegated to option status for 1972, and the car was past its best. Nevertheless, the W-30 performance package on the 4-4-2 was worth having, and the Cool Air 455 V8 (RIGHT) gave 300bhp even by the new way of reckoning power figures.

BELOW: The 1972 Pontiac Firebird also waned in popularity as the Muscle Car era was coming to an end.

Once past the shock of discovering that indignity, however, an Oldsmobile buyer might have recognized a few familiar items elsewhere on the options list. Although the standard hardware was a 350 V8 with 160bhp in two-barrel form or 180bhp with a four-barrel carburetor, the 455 big-block was still listed in four-barrel form, now with 270bhp. As last year's *gross* figure had been 340bhp, the engine hadn't lost all that much. Even more interesting was the W-30 performance package, which brought a fiberglass hood with functional air scoops, a limited-slip rear axle, and a 300bhp factory-blueprinted Cool Air 455. A W-30 would reach 60mph in a respectable 6.6 seconds and could still run quarter-miles in the mid-14s at 92mph.

Also listed for 1972 was a Hurst/Olds package, available like the 4-4-2 as an option on the Cutlass line. Decals and other appearance goodies were undoubtedly a major fac-tor in its appeal, but the 270bhp 455 gave it real credibility. Not up to the Hurst/Olds collaborations of earlier times, it nevertheless ran quarter-miles in 15.2 seconds and would hit 60mph from rest in well under 7 seconds. Oldsmobile shipped 629 cars with the package before the season was finished.

Pontiac, too, retained their 455 for 1972, along with the 400. The GTO package wasn't available on convertibles, and the GTO Judge had also gone. Only minor changes distinguished the 1972 Pontiac intermediates from the 1971s, although the performance models could be ordered with a pair of spoiler options. The GTO power options were 250bhp from the 400, 250bhp with automatic transmission from the 455, and 300bhp from the High Output 455 with a stick shift. A 1972 GTO hardtop with the 300bhp option wasn't a spectacular performer, though, not least because it had put on weight. Mid-15s

LEFT: AMC's 390 engine in their 1972 AMX.

The Pontiac Firebird had a bad year in 1972, although performance from the top models hadn't been too badly hit. The Trans Am (RIGHT) came as standard with the 300bhp 455 motor, and still looked good with its blue racing stripes on the white bodywork.

were about par for the quarter-mile, and the car took more than 7 seconds to reach 60mph. By comparison with the herd of lesser 1972 models, the GTO was still fast, but it couldn't come near most of its illustrious fore-bears. Production dropped again.

The Firebird had a terrible year, which wasn't helped by a long strike at the GM plant which assembled both Firebirds and Chevrolet Camaros. Pontiac dropped all sticker prices on the Firebird range, and settled for mini-mal changes over the '71s. As before, there were four Fire-bird models, the Formula and Trans Am being the per-formance-oriented editions. Interesting engine options started with the 400 in 250bhp form (there was also a 175bhp version), but the 300bhp 455 was the engine to go for. It was optional in regular Firebirds and standard in the Trans Am.

The Trans Am came as standard with a four-speed manual transmission and a Hurst shifter, but the major-ity of the 1286 cars built had the optional automatic. In line with the times, Pontiac didn't offer any choice of axle ratios (although those for the manual and automatic editions differed), but the Trans Am once again came with a Safe-T-Track limited-slip differential as standard. It was an expensive car, but still worth it: 60mph came up in just 5.4 seconds on the street, and the car would turn quarters in just under 14 seconds. In 1972, the Trans Am was the cream of the crop.

Chevrolet

After two years in second place, Chevrolet once again out-sold Ford in 1972. While that was good news in one re-spect, it didn't reflect on the quality of the division's Muscle Car offerings. This year, they were cut to the bone.

Buyers who wanted a high-performance Chevrolet didn't really have to look any farther than the Chevelle line. Two-doors still had 112 inches between their axles, although styling was all new this year. The hot one was the SS 454 Malibu hardtop coupé, equipped with the LS-5 option 454 V8. Last year's gross output had been listed as 365bhp; this year, the net output was claimed to be 270bhp. Power was undoubtedly down, but the SS 454 was still among the quickest of 1972's models.

More important for sales in 1972 was the Chevelle-based "Heavy Chevy," a sort of budget SS without any real performance but with plenty of street appeal. Its 175bhp 350 V8 wasn't to be taken seriously, but the 240bhp 402 option did provide a little more excitement.

The Nova had bowed out of the performance market in 1971, although Chevrolet still marketed an SS edition with a 200bhp four-barrel 350. Strip figures made clear that they weren't serious, however, because a '72 Nova SS needed nearly 15.5 seconds to run the quarter-mile and achieved a trap speed of only 88.4mph.

The Camaro, affected by the same strike as the Fire-bird, had its worst-ever year, and 1972 would prove to be

the last year for the big-block engines and the SS option. Chevrolet still offered a Z-28 edition, now with 255bhp from its 350 V8; next down the list was the 240bhp 402; but after that power dropped below 200bhp and didn't put the Camaro into the serious performance class.

AMC

Even though AMC were clinging ever more tightly to their small sedans, they still offered performance enthusiasts something worth having in the shape of the Javelin AMX. Visually, this was very much the same as last season's model, although the tail-lamps had been redesigned. The standard motor was now a 150bhp 304, but the optional 360 gave 175bhp with two barrels, 195bhp with four barrels, or a more interesting 220bhp with four barrels and a dual exhaust system. The 401 V8 was still available, but its compression had been lowered and it came with an advertised 255bhp, which wasn't enough to make the Javelin AMX into a winner. Quarter-miles took more than 16 seconds this year, and the car needed well over eight seconds to reach 60mph from rest.

However, AMC still knew how to make a car look good. The optional "Go" package for the Javelin AMX added racing stripes and hood decals, Cowl-Air induction with the inevitable hood scoop, heavy-duty suspension with fatter tires, and a special instrument pack. The fact that AMC were still taking part in NASCAR racing – though with the Matador sedan rather than the Javelin – must also have helped the company's high-performance image. But that was all it was for '72 – an image.

The SS appearance package made the 1972 Chevrolet Chevelle look muscular, even if it had one of the lesser engines under its hood (RIGHT). Most powerful option was the 454 V8, with 270bhp, shown here below right.

BELOW: The 1972 AMC Javelin AMX

Muscle Car Choice – 1972

Compacts
Chevrolet Nova SS 350
Dodge Demon 340
Plymouth Duster 340

Ponycars
AMC Javelin AMX 401
Chevrolet Camaro Z-28
Ford Mustang Mach 1
(with 351 option)
Pontiac Firebird Formula
455
Pontiac Firebird Trans Am

Intermediates
Buick GS-455
Chevrolet Malibu SS 454
Ford Gran Torino Sport
(with 351 option)
Oldsmobile 4-4-2
(with 455 option)
Plymouth Road Runner
Pontiac GTO

1973
A Sales Blip

Some people would argue that 1972 had been the last year for real Muscle Cars, and that the 1973 introductions didn't include anything of interest to muscle fans. That isn't quite true, though. Although the numbers of genuine high-performance cars had dropped, Detroit still offered a handful of models which were way out in front of the rest of the herd in terms of their accelerative ability. They weren't as fast as many of their 1960s predecessors, but they were aimed squarely at that small sector of the market for whom the ability to outdrag other new cars still mattered. Of course, meeting older performance models at a stoplights drag-race could cause some embarrassment. . . .

It is also undeniable that the legacy of the high-performance era was still around to affect the way some of the 1973 cars looked. There were plenty of sheep in wolves' clothing: sporty-looking cars with all the right decals and other addenda but without the once-essential ingredient of a muscular V8 under their hoods.

Emissions regulations tightened still further for 1973, with the inevitable result that power outputs took another tumble. As if that wasn't enough, new safety regulations demanded bumpers capable of withstanding a 5mph impact without damage to the main body of the car. In most cases, the new bumpers not only looked hideous but also added a great deal of weight – the last thing the cars needed at a time when engine outputs were also on the decrease.

Strangely enough, 1973 was a boom year for new-car sales in the U.S.A. In the midst of all these engineering changes which were making new cars less and less attractive, the American buying public flocked to the showrooms in unprecedented numbers. The few Muscle Cars which remained available this year sold in quite encouraging numbers. But next year would reverse all that as an oil embargo took its toll, both on overall new-car sales and on the popularity of gas-guzzling Muscle Cars.

Buick, Oldsmobile, and Pontiac

General Motors' Buick, Oldsmobile, and Pontiac divisions still fielded a handful of Muscle Cars for 1973, although it was clear that their hearts weren't really in the performance business any more. All except for Pontiac's Firebird were intermediates, which meant that they all shared the same new "A-body" which arrived with that season's models. To meet new (and anticipated) Federal safety regulations, raked-pillar "Colonnade" styling replaced hardtops, and convertibles were not offered.

Buick didn't offer a GS any more, but they retained the model line in the shape of a Gran Sport option on the 112-inch-wheelbase Century coupé. This was distinguished by discreet decals, blacked-out headlamp surrounds and grille, fat wheels and tires – and by the only manual transmission option in the Buick catalog for 1973. Gran Sport power options started as low as 150bhp (from a two-barrel 350 V8), but started to get interesting with the 225bhp 455, which could be ordered on any of the Century coupés. Exclusive to the Gran Sport, however, was the 270bhp Stage I 455, which had camshaft, carburation, and air cleaner changes: a Posi-Traction limited-slip rear end also came as part of the Stage I package.

Few 1973 cars were quicker than a Stage I 455 Gran Sport, which says a lot about the way performance standards had fallen in the early 1970s. The car took 8.9 seconds to reach 60mph from rest and needed 15.3 seconds to run the quarter-mile, with a trap speed of just 90mph. Only 728 customers bothered to buy this top-performing Buick before the 1973 season ended.

Oldsmobile seemed to have lost interest altogether. The 4-4-2 package survived as an option on the newly restyled Cutlass Colonnade intermediates, but it was more about appearance than performance. There was no hot W-30 package to be had, and not even a fiberglass hood was listed among the options. As a Muscle Car maker, Oldsmobile was finished.

Pontiac was still trying hard, although its performance leader was now the Firebird and the intermediates were more like token performance cars. Restyled along with the Buick and Oldsmobile intermediates, the Pontiac Le Mans range remained the basis on which a GTO could be ordered – although buyers had to hunt hard for it in the options lists. The GTO came with decals, a heavy-duty suspension, and a 400-cubic-inch V8 which couldn't muster more than 230bhp. Only 4806 Pontiac buyers bothered, and the sales force was much more interested in promoting what Pontiac hoped might be the next new thing – a car which combined performance with luxury.

The concept wasn't new, of course. In fact, it was

ABOVE: The stylish, but emasculated, 1973 Ford Mustang SportsRoof.

As the decals on the front fender proclaim (RIGHT), this is a Pontiac GTO with the 400-cubic-inch V8 motor. But the GTO was now just an option package on the Le Mans line, and the car looked fat and bloated. Performance was nothing special, either.

derived from the formula which had made imported sports sedans – particuarly from Mercedes-Benz and BMW – so popular in recent years. Pontiac called their new Le Mans derivative the Grand Am, attempting in that name to encapsulate the car's mix of Grand Prix luxury with Trans Am performance. Unfortunately, the latter part of that combination was a disappointment. Despite packing a 250bhp edition of the 455 big-block V8, the Grand Am needed 7.9 seconds to reach 60mph and took 15.7 seconds to run the quarter-mile. It didn't really satisfy any group of customers and was not a great seller.

It might have been the lackluster peformance of these intermediates which turned Pontiac buyers toward the Firebird and Trans Am models this year. The performance-oriented Formula, and the Trans Am itself, both sold much better than in 1972, with Formula sales nearly doubled and Trans Am sales nearly four times higher than their 1972 total.

The Formula could be ordered with the 455 High Output V8 which was standard in the Trans Am, although the accompanying hood scoop was now blocked off to meet emissions regulations, and output was down to 250bhp. However, early in 1973 a 310bhp Super Duty 455 option was introduced. In an age of dropping power outputs, one which had increased by such a margin was immediately of interest to Muscle Car fans. Again, it could be had in both Formula and Trans Am Firebirds, although unfortunately it lasted only a couple of months in this form before it was fitted with a new camshaft to meet emissions control guidelines and was de-rated to 290bhp. Even then, it was a formidable powerplant for its time.

Dodge and Plymouth

Dodge's Muscle Cars for 1973 came from the same three ranges as last season's models. However, the Demon coupé had been renamed a Dart Sport after customers with curious sensibilities objected to the earlier name. More important was that power was down once again, and the hot Dodges really weren't all that hot any more.

Best-seller was still the compact coupé, which still had the 340 small-block V8 in its hottest performance guise. In fact, sales of 11,315 made the 1973 Dart Sport 340 more popular than last year's Demon 340, which had sold just 8750 units. The 1973 car still came with 240bhp, but weight had gone up and it wasn't quite as fast as the 1972 Demon.

That 240bhp 340 V8 was also the hottest option in 1973's Challenger, Dodge's 110-inch-wheelbase ponycar. This year, customers created Rallye editions by specifying an option package, as the Rallye wasn't a separate model any longer. Dodge were probably well pleased with increased Challenger sales this year – up to some 32,500 from last year's figure of around 26,500 – although most of these cars had the 150bhp 318 V8 which wasn't of any interest to performance fans. The 340 wasn't all that exciting, either, but Muscle Car fans probably experienced a momentary thrill when they heard that a 360 V8 was to be made optional at mid-season. They need hardly have bothered: the 360 had been introduced because extra capacity was the only way to keep power up in the face of tightening emissions control regulations. The new motor did have 245bhp as against the 340's 240bhp, but the difference was barely noticeable.

Ford still offered the Mustang with 351 power for 1973, but the actual output was now down as low as 156bhp. This convertible model (BELOW LEFT AND RIGHT) looked great, but was just a shadow of earlier 351s in the performance stakes.

Largest of the Dodge muscle machines for '73 was still the Charger, which had the same 115-inch-wheelbase body as in 1972 but had picked up some front and rear cosmetic changes together with enlarged rear quarter-windows to eliminate an irritating blind spot. This year, the optional Rallye package boasted loud side-stripes, a pinned-down hood with a power bulge, anti-sway bars front and rear, fat tires with raised white lettering, and special instrumentation. Charger power options included the 400 V8 in both 175bhp and 260bhp forms, but the most interesting of the lot was the old faithful 440 V8, now running in low compression form on low-lead gasoline but still offering 280bhp. This one would heave a Charger to 60mph from rest in 7.4 seconds, and promised quarter-miles in the low 15s.

In NASCAR events, driver Richard Petty was now back full-time with Dodge, and he campaigned a '73 Charger with considerable success. That year, he claimed victory in six events, including the Daytona 500.

The picture at Plymouth was much the same as it was at Dodge. Best sales were achieved by the Duster 340, which found slightly more buyers than it had in '72; a Road Runner coupé kept intermediate Muscle Car sales alive; and the hot 'Cuda derivative of the Barracuda pony-car did even better than last year.

The Duster 340 was pretty much the same car as it had been for 1972, and was still advertised with 240bhp, although those horses had to propel a slightly heavier automobile than before. The Road Runner had definitely taken a turn for the worse, however, with new frontal styling brought about by its 5mph impact bumpers which did nothing for its looks. Standard power was down this

year to a ludicrous 170bhp from a 318 V8, although most buyers chose the 240bhp 340 option. Above that were more promising 400 and 440 V8s, with 260bhp and 280bhp respectively. Unfortunately, relatively few buyers among the 19,056 who bought Road Runners in 1973 wanted these high-performance options. Plymouth, comparing this year's sales total with last year's Road Runner figure of just 7628, must have concluded that they had the balance about right in '73. However, it was also true that the Road Runner was one of a rapidly dwindling number of cars which even pretended to have high performance, and this had no doubt helped sales as much as anything else.

Plymouth dropped the six-cylinder Barracuda for 1973, and the entry-level model now had the 318 V8 as standard. The 340 was optional, and standard in the 'Cuda. Just as with Dodge's Challenger, the 340 gave way to a 360 at mid-season, although performance remained unaffected. Once again, the upturn in sales – which affected the regular Barracuda line as well – must have encouraged Plymouth's planners to assume that they had got the model and options mixes about right. High performance just wasn't in demand any longer, and in fact sales were better without it.

Ford and Mercury

Performance still had a low priority for Ford and its Mercury division, although there were models which still had the trappings of performance. The Mustang, which was to receive a disappointing restyle in 1974, could still be had in Mach 1 guise, and there were enough options to make a Torino look tough for the street.

The Rally Sport package dresses this Chevrolet Camaro (ABOVE AND LEFT) to look good, but even the 350 V8 option didn't offer more than 175bhp.

(ABOVE RIGHT) The 1973 AMC Javelin AMX.

**Muscle Car
Choice – 1973**

Compacts
Dodge Dart Sport 340
Plymouth Duster 340

Ponycars
AMC Javelin AMX 401
Chevrolet Camaro Z-28
Pontiac Firebird Formula
(with 455 option)
Pontiac Firebird Trans Am

Intermediates
Buick Gran Sport
(with 455 option)
Chevrolet Chevelle
(with 454 option)
Dodge Charger
(with 440 option)
Plymouth Road Runner
(with 400 or 440 option)
Pontiac Grand Am

Ford's ponycar was cosmetically very similar to the 1972 models, although new bumpers designed to meet the 5mph impact rules were an instant recognition feature. The Mach 1 came with competition suspension as standard and with the option of a scooped hood, but the 302 V8 with just 136bhp was standard, and buyers couldn't get anything more accelerative than a 351 Cleveland V8, which this year had no more than 156bhp. No-one doubted that the 1973 Mach 1 was all show and very little go.

Much the same had already happened to the Torino, although the fastback SportsRoof body was still around for 1973 and could be equipped with the 429 big-block. As in 1972, however, the motor was tuned for smooth progress rather than fierce acceleration, and its 201bhp didn't really deliver. Some Torinos were dressed to look like performance cars, though, with racing mirrors, mag style wheels, raised-letter tires, and blacked-out lower body panels.

Over at Mercury, the Cougar had lost the most powerful of last year's 351 options. It came as standard with a 168bhp 351, or with a more interesting four-barrel 264bhp 351 CJ option. Both hardtop and convertible models were available, but 1973 would be the last year for the Cougar in this form.

Chevrolet
GM's best-selling division clung rather half-heartedly to a pair of Muscle Car contenders for 1973. Only the Camaro in Z-28 form and the Chevelle with its big 454 option were really worth considering for buyers who wanted hot machinery this year.

The Camaro range for '73 had been stripped of all its big-block options and no longer included SS models; instead there was a top-of-the-range Camaro LT, with a collection of lukewarm V8 options. Far and away the most powerful was the 245bhp 350 motor available only in the Z-28, but it was 10bhp down on last year and was being asked to move a heavier car, so the effect on performance was predictable. Chevrolet made a smart move by dropping the price of the Z-28 package, however, and they were rewarded by an increase in sales. This year's total for Z-28s was the best since 1969.

It was a sad reflection on what emissions controls had done to the big-blocks that the 1973 version of the 454 V8 had the same 245bhp as the 350 small-block. It could still be had in the Chevelle, where it was the hottest option, but buyers had to manage without the SS package. The weight of the 1973 Chevelle had also increased considerably, so that a 454-powered Chevelle wasn't anything like the car it had once been.

AMC
AMC refused to give up on Muscle Cars just yet, although a quick look at the other models they were offering for 1973 showed that cars like the Javelin AMX weren't likely to form part of their long-term strategy. This year's model was very largely a carryover from 1972, tricked out with new rear lights. Top option – and the only one with any real performance interest – was the 401 V8, still advertised with 255bhp. The '73s weren't as quick as earlier AMX 401s, with quarters in the mid-15s at 90mph and zero to 60mph times of 7.7 seconds. Even so, the public bought more AMXs than they had done in 1972.

1974

The End

It's interesting to speculate how long the Muscle Cars might have lingered if the oil embargo of 1973-1974 hadn't so radically changed American perceptions of the automobile. It had been clear by the end of the 1972 season that the era of big sales for brutally powerful cars was over, but the upturn in sales which 1973's few remaining Muscle Cars experienced could well have persuaded manufacturers to hang on in there for a little while longer.

However, politics intervened. On October 19, 1973, Saudi Arabia (followed by the remaining OPEC nations) placed an embargo on oil supplies to the U.S.A. That embargo was finally lifted on March 13, 1974, but the intervening five months had witnessed fuel shortages which had made quite clear to car makers and car buyers alike that there was no place in the future for the gas-guzzlers they had been used to. It took some time for the new and more fuel-efficient models to filter through to the showrooms, but the middle of the 1970s saw a complete turnaround in the American automobile.

It was that focus on gas-guzzlers which finally killed off the Muscle Cars. At a time when gas was in short supply, big-block V8s which consumed fuel at the rate of one gallon to every nine or ten miles even when driven carefully were not what the public wanted. They made that quite clear by refusing to buy 1974's Muscle Car offerings. And the makers responded to this collapse in the market by dropping those models for 1975.

General Motors

The General still offered a handful of Muscle Cars for 1974. Chevrolet had their Camaro Z-28 and their Chevelle 454; Buick's Gran Sport was still interesting with its big-block 455 options; and Pontiac's Grand Am and Firebird Trans Am offered two different approaches to the performance theme.

This year's Chevrolet Camaro and Pontiac Firebird ponycars both had revised front and rear styling. The Z-28 Camaro still came with its 245bhp 350 small-block, and the Firebird still had its 250bhp 455 big-block, while a 290bhp 455 was optional. Despite all the odds, sales of GM's hot ponycars actually increased this year, but Chevrolet decided not to tarnish the image of the Z-28 by issuing a less powerful model for 1975 and withdrew the

model at the end of the 1974 season. Pontiac, however, encouraged by Trans Am sales which were nearly double those of 1973, kept the model right through the 1970s even though performance continued to drop off.

Sales of Pontiac's Grand Am nose-dived this season, and the model didn't last beyond the end of 1975. As before, top performance option was the 250bhp 455. Buick, meanwhile, had to contend with a Gran Sport which was even heavier than the 1973 model. Coupled to lower-powered V8s (top option was now a 255bhp Stage I 455), the cars simply didn't go as well. Gran Sports disappeared for 1975.

Ford and Mercury

Already lost to the performance world, Ford and Mercury showed that they didn't care at all during 1974. The new Mustang II didn't have a single V8 on its options list, and the best it could manage was a German-built V6 which didn't make it into a high-performance car despite the sporty appearance of some versions. A 302 V8 would be added for 1975, but it didn't change the character of the Mustang II one little bit. As far as the Torino was concerned, nothing more powerful than a 170bhp 400 V8 was on offer for '74.

Mercury transferred the Cougar name to their Montego line this year, which meant that the model put on a huge amount of weight as compared to its 1973 incarnation. With this kind of handicap, even the optional 254bhp 351 Cleveland V8 couldn't make a 1974 Cougar XR7 into the sort of car which appealed to performance enthusiasts.

Dodge and Plymouth

The compacts from Chrysler's Dodge and Plymouth Divisions took on larger V8s to offset the effect of tightening emissions control regulations. They remained the best-selling Muscle Car lines this season, and were kept in production for 1975. However, Plymouth's Road Runner and Dodge's Challenger disappeared at the end of 1974, and the 1975 Dodge Charger moved out of the serious performance market and into the personal luxury sector.

This year, the 360 V8 was the mainstay of those Dodges and Plymouths which had any performance pretensions. In four-barrel form for the Plymouth Duster

360, it had 245bhp and gave the car 0 to 60mph times of 8.2 seconds and quarter-miles in the high 15s. Road Runners and Challengers also had the 360 as an option, although it didn't make either into a fast car. Best option in the Charger was a 275bhp 440, although Richard Petty was still driving his '73 Charger in NASCAR events, which said something about the '74 models that no Dodge advertising was going to admit. Petty had another successful season, claiming 10 victories for Dodge and winning the drivers' championship.

AMC

Nineteen seventy-four was the last season for the Javelin AMX, which was still rated at 255bhp with its 401 V8 despite tighter emissions regulations. AMC had managed to even out this year's losses by fitting a different carburetor and a dual exhaust system. However, despite their efforts to retain some muscle, this was to be the last year for the company's ponycar contender, and the 401 disappeared along with the rest of the line at the end of the 1974 season.

The Dodge Challenger (LEFT) was in its final season during 1974, and could offer nothing more stirring than a 245bhp 360 V8. The Charger from the same stable, however, did recall happier times with its 440 Magnum V8, even though no more than 275bhp were available (BELOW LEFT). Side stripes still mattered in the performance market for 1974, such as it was.

Muscle Car Choice – 1974

Compacts
Dodge Dart Sport 360
Plymouth Duster 360

Ponycars
AMC Javelin AMX 401
Chevrolet Camaro Z-28
Pontiac Firebird Trans Am

Intermediates
Buick Gran Sport
(with 455 option)
Chevrolet Chevelle
(with 454 option)
Plymouth Road runner
(with 400 or 440 option)

Epilogue

So, is the Muscle Car just a historical curio? Any answer to that question can only be a cautious one. Many of the cars themselves still survive in the hands of collectors and enthusiasts, and a number of the competition versions are still run on occasions at appropriate events. Their owners would mostly hate to think of them as nothing more than museum pieces.

What is undeniable, however, is that Detroit had stopped building Muscle Cars like these by the mid-1970s. The American manufacturers didn't get back into the high-performance game until a decade and a half later, when pressure from certain European imports in the late 1980s obliged them to do so. A new generation of high-performance cars is already appearing, but it wouldn't be right to call them Muscle Cars. Their character is totally different, due to the increasingly sophisticated high-technology driving aids, which reduce the driver's risk of making an error; and they are much too expensive for the average enthusiast to buy. While these new performance models accelerate fast, handle well, and stop reliably, they simply don't offer the same raw excitement as the best of the old-style Muscle Cars. . . .

The last of the boom years before the Muscle Car market collapsed had been 1970, which is represented by this Dodge Coronet R/T (BELOW), now the property of an enthusiast in England. It was a year when decals (RIGHT) were essential ingredients in the Muscle Car, but within four years decals were all that was left.

Index

ACKNOWLEDGMENTS

The author and publisher would like to thank David Eldred for designing the book, Stephen Small the editor and picture researcher, Susan Brown for production, Ron Watson for compiling the index, and the following individuals and agencies for providing the photographs:

American Car World/Daniel B. Lyons, pages: 16(bottom), 17(both), 164(top), 165, 166(bottom)

American Car World/Tony Beadle, pages: 198-9, 200, 201(bottom), 217(top)

Auto-Foto/William L. Bailey, pages: 51

Brompton Books, pages: 9(both), 25(bottom), 36(top), 37, 85, 148(top), 148-9, 175, 176

Brompton Books/Nicky Wright, pages: 10(top), 48(both), 56, 57(bottom), 58, 59(bottom), 60-1, 86(both), 87(both), 107(both), 108-9, 110, 111, 112-3, 117(top), 118(both), 119, 120-1, 168(top), 170-1(all three), 178, 190-1(all three), 193(both), 205, 214, 215

Neill Bruce, pages: 49(both), 75(bottom), 76(top), 95(top), 132(bottom), 133, 179, 180-1

Colin Burnham, pages: 12, 74(bottom), 76(bottom), 96(bottom)

Classic American, pages: 211(top), 216(bottom), 220-1

GM/Pontiac Motor Division, pages: 10(bottom), 11, 29, 30-1, 33(bottom), 41(top), 63(bottom), 78-9(both), 80-1, 104(both), 105(bottom), 135, 136(top & middle), 138, 139(top), 164(bottom), 196, 213(bottom)

Phil Kunz, pages: 13(top), 14-15, 18, 19, 21(both), 26, 27, 28(both), 36(bottom), 38(both), 39(both), 41(bottom), 42, 43(all three), 44, 46-7(both), 52-3(both), 54-5, 55(top), 57(top), 59(top), 62(top), 63(top), 64, 65(both), 67(top), 68-9, 69(top), 70(top), 71(top), 72-3(both), 75(top), 77, 84,88, 89(top), 90, 91, 94, 95(bottom), 96(top), 97(both), 99(both), 100(bottom), 101, 102-3, 103(top), 105(top), 106(both), 116, 117(bottom), 122, 123(both), 124, 128-9(both), 130(both), 131, 132(top), 134(all three), 136(bottom), 137, 139(bottom), 140-1(all three), 142(both), 143(both), 144, 145(both), 149(top), 150(both), 151(both), 152, 153(both), 154(both), 155(both), 157(top), 160, 162, 163(both), 166(top), 167, 168(bottom), 172(both), 173(both), 174(both), 177(both), 183, 184, 185(both), 186(both), 187(both), 188(top), 189(top), 192, 194(both), 197(both), 201(both), 206, 207(top), 211(bottom), 219(bottom)

Lifefile/Jerry Heasley, pages: 20, 24, 33(top), 50, 66-7

Lifefile/Jim Smart, pages: 25(top), 45(both), 100(top), 115(top), 195(top)

National Motor Museum, England, pages: 13(bottom), 70(bottom), 74(top), 82-3, 158-9, 161(bottom)

Nicky Wright/National Motor Museum, pages: 1, 2-3, 4-5, 6, 7(both), 8, 16(top), 23(both), 34-5, 54(top), 89(bottom), 92-3, 102(top), 114-15, 125, 126-7, 146-7, 156-7, 161(top), 162(top), 188-9, 195(bottom), 207(bottom), 208, 209, 210(bottom), 219(top), 211(top), 213(top)